How to SUCCEED in the Christian Life

R. A. TORREY

Publisher's Note

*This updated version of **How To Succeed In The Christian Life** is offered to our readers in the sincere hope that it will bless many lives. All revisions were prayerfully considered in order to retain R.A. Torrey's original message and flavor.*

HOW TO SUCCEED IN THE CHRISTIAN LIFE

*Dedicated to
the thousands in many
lands who have accepted Christ.*

CONTENTS

INTRODUCTION

New Christians need a book that will outline basic principles of their faith so they will enjoy complete success in their new life. Since I could not find such a book, I wrote one myself. This book aims to tell the new convert just what he needs to know most. I hope that pastors, evangelists, and other Christian workers will find it a good book to give young converts. I hope it will also prove helpful to many who have been Christians for a long time but have not made the headway in their Christian life they desire.

Chapter 1

BEGINNING RIGHT

Beginning the Christian life with a solid, correct foundation influences the success of the remainder of a Christian's life. However, if someone has started life with Jesus, yet is unsure of their foundation, it is simple to strengthen it with solid Christian principles.

Receive Jesus As Savior

We are told the right beginning for the Christian life in John 1:12, "But as many as received Him, to them gave He power to become the sons of God, even to them that believe on His name." The right way to begin the Christian life is by receiving Jesus Christ. He immediately gives power to become a child of God to anyone who receives Him.

If the reader of this book was the most wicked man on earth, and then he received Jesus Christ, that very instant he would become a child of God. God promises this in the most unqualified way in the verse quoted above. No one can become a child of God any other way. No man, no matter how carefully he has been raised, no matter how well he has been sheltered from the vices and evils of this world, is a child of God until he receives Jesus Christ. We are "children of God by faith in Christ Jesus" (Galatians 3:26) and in no other way.

What does it mean to receive Jesus Christ? It means to take Christ to be all God offers Him to be to everybody. Jesus Christ is God's gift. "For God so loved the world that He gave His only begotten Son that whosoever believeth in Him should not perish but have everlasting life" (John 3:16).

Some accept this wondrous gift of God. Everyone who does accept this gift becomes a child of God. Many others refuse this wondrous gift of God, and everyone who refuses this gift perishes. He condemns himself. "He that believeth on Him is not condemned: but he that believeth not is condemned already, because he hath not believed in the name of the only begotten Son of God" (John 3:18).

Jesus Is Our Sin-Bearer

What does God offer His Son to be to us?

First of all, *God offers Jesus to us to be our sin-bearer.* We have all sinned. There is not a man or woman, a boy or girl, who has not sinned. "Even the righteousness of God which is by faith of Jesus Christ unto all and upon all them that believe: for there is no difference: For all have sinned, and come short of the glory of God" (Romans 3:22,23). If any of us say that we have not sinned, we are deceiving ourselves and giving the lie to God. "If we say that we have no sin, we deceive ourselves, and the truth is not in us. If we say that we have not sinned, we make Him a liar, and His Word is not in us" (1 John 1:8,10). Each of us must bear our own sin, or someone else must bear it in our place. If we were to bear our own sins, it would mean we must be banished forever from the presence of God, for God is holy. "God is light, and in Him is no darkness at all" (1 John 1:5).

But God Himself has provided another to take responsibility for our sins so that we do not need to bear them ourselves. This sin-bearer is God's own Son, Jesus Christ, "For He hath made Him to be sin for us, who knew no sin; that we might be made the righteousness of God in Him" (2 Corinthians 5:21).

When Jesus Christ died upon the cross of Calvary, He redeemed us from the curse of the law by being made a curse in our stead. "Christ hath redeemed us from the curse of the law, being made a curse for us: for it is written, Cursed is every one that hangeth on a tree" (Galatians 3:13). To receive Christ then is to believe this testimony of God about His Son, to believe that Jesus Christ did bear our sins in His own body on the cross. "Who His own self bare our sins in His own body on the tree, that we, being dead to sins, should live unto righteousness: by whose stripes ye were healed" (1 Peter 2:24). We know we can trust God to forgive all our sins because Jesus Christ has borne them in our place.

"All we like sheep have gone astray; we have turned every one to his own way; and the Lord hath laid on Him the iniquity of us all" (Isaiah 53:6). Our own good works, past, present, or future, have nothing to do with the forgiveness of our sins. Our sins are forgiven, not because of any good works we do, they are forgiven because of the atoning work of Christ on the cross of Calvary in our place. If we rest in this atoning work, we will do good works. But our good works will be the outcome of our being saved and our believing on Christ as our sin-bearer. Our good works will not be the ground of our salvation, but the result of our salvation and the proof of it.

We must be very careful not to believe in our good works at all as the basis of salvation. We are not forgiven because of Christ's death *and our good works*; we are forgiven solely and entirely because of Christ's death. To see this clearly is the right beginning of the true Christian life.

Our Deliverer From Sin

God offers Jesus to us as our deliverer from the power of sin. Jesus not only died, He rose again. Today He is a living Savior. He has all power in heaven and on earth. "And Jesus came and spake unto them, saying, All power is given unto Me in heaven and in earth" (Matthew 28:18). He has the power to keep the weakest sinner from falling. "Now in Him that is able to keep you from falling, and to present you faultless before the presence of His glory with exceeding joy" (Jude 24). He is able to save not only from the worst but elevate to the highest all who come unto the Father through Him. "Wherefore He is able also to save them to the uttermost that come unto God by Him, seeing He ever liveth to make intercession for them" (Hebrews 7:25). "If the Son therefore shall make you free, ye shall be free indeed" (John 8:36).

To receive Jesus is to believe what God tells us in His Word about Him: to believe that He did rise from the dead; to believe that He does now live; to believe that He has the power to keep us from falling; to believe that He has the power to keep us from the power of sin day by day. Then, we must trust Him to do what He has said.

This is the secret of daily victory over sin. If we try to fight sin in our own strength, we are bound to fail. If we look up to the risen Christ to keep us every day and every hour, He will keep us. Through the crucified Christ, we get deliverance from the guilt of sin, our sins are all blotted out, and we are free from all condemnation. But it is through the risen Christ that we get daily victory over the power of sin.

Some receive Christ as a sin-bearer and thus find pardon, but they do not get beyond that. Thus their life is one of daily failure. Others receive Him as their risen Savior also, and they experience victory over sin. To begin right, we must take Him not only as our sin-bearer, and thus find pardon; we must also take Him as our risen Savior, our daily deliverer from the power of sin.

Jesus Is Lord

God offers Jesus to us, not only as our sin-bearer and our deliverer from the power of sin, but He also offers Him to us as our Lord and King. We read in Acts 2:36, "Let all the house of Israel know assuredly, that God hath made that same Jesus, whom ye have crucified, both Lord and Christ." Lord means divine Master, and Christ means anointed King.

To receive Jesus is to take Him as our divine Master, as the One to whom we yield the absolute confidence of our intellects. Believe He is the One in whose Word we can believe absolutely, the One in whom we will believe though many of the wisest of men may question or deny the truth of His teachings. As our King, we gladly yield absolute control of our lives to Him, so that the question from this time on is: *What would my King Jesus have me do?* A correct beginning involves an unconditional surrender to the lordship and kingship of Jesus.

The failure to realize that Jesus is Lord and King, as well as Savior, has led to many a false start in the Christian life. We begin with Him as our Savior, our sin-bearer, and our deliverer from the power of sin. We must not end with Him merely as Savior, we must know Him as Lord and King. There is nothing more important in a right beginning of Christian life than an unconditional surrender, both of thoughts and conduct, to Jesus. Say from your heart and say it again and again, *"All for*

Jesus."

Surrender Your Life To Jesus

Many fail because they shrink back from this entire surrender. They wish to serve Jesus with half their heart, part of themselves, and part of their possessions. To hold back anything from Jesus means a wretched life of stumbling and failure.

The life of entire surrender is a joyous life all along the way. If you have never done it before, go alone with God today, get down on your knees, and say, "All for Jesus," and mean it. Say it very earnestly, say it from the bottom of your heart. Stay there until you realize what it means and what you are doing. It is a wondrous step forward when one really takes it.

If you have taken it already, take it again, take it often. It always has fresh meaning and brings fresh blessing. In this absolute surrender is found the key to all truth. "If any man will do His will, he shall know of the doctrine, whether it be of God, or whether I speak of Myself" (John 7:17). In this absolute surrender is found the secret of power in prayer. (See 1 John 3:22.) In this absolute surrender is found the supreme condition of receiving the Holy Spirit. "And we are His witnesses of these things; and so is also the Holy Ghost, whom God hath given to them that obey Him" (Acts 5:32).

Taking Christ as your Lord and King involves obedience to His will as far as you know it in each small detail of life. There are those who tell us they have taken Christ as their Lord and King who at the same time are disobeying Him daily. They disobey Him in business, domestic life, social life, and personal conduct. These people are deceiving themselves. You have not taken Jesus as your Lord and King if you are not striving to obey Him in everything each day. He Himself says, "Why call ye Me Lord, Lord and do not the things which I say?" (Luke 6:46).

To sum it all up, the right way to begin the Christian life is to accept Jesus Christ as your sin-bearer. Trust God to forgive your sins because Jesus Christ died in your place. You must accept Him as your risen Savior who lives to make intercession for you and who has complete power to keep you. Trust Him to keep you from day to day, and accept Him as your Lord and King to whom you surrender absolute control of your thoughts and life.

This is the right beginning, the only right beginning of the Christian life. If you have made this beginning, all that follows will be comparatively easy. If you have not made this beginning, make it now.

Chapter 2

CONFESSING CHRIST

Once you have begun the Christian life correctly by taking the proper attitude toward Christ in a private transaction between Himself and yourself, your next step is to make an open confession of the relationship that now exists between you and Jesus Christ. Jesus says in Matthew 10:32, "Whosoever therefore shall confess Me before men, him will I confess also before My Father which is in heaven." He demands a public confession. He demands it for your sake. This is the path of blessing.

Many attempt to be disciples of Jesus without telling the world. No one has ever succeeded in that attempt. To be a secret disciple means to be no disciple at all. If one really has received Christ, he cannot keep it to himself. "For out of the abundance of the heart the mouth speaketh" (Matthew 12:34).

Are You A Closet Christian?

So important is the public confession of Christ

that Paul puts it first in his statement of the conditions of salvation. He says, "If thou shalt *confess with thy mouth* the Lord Jesus, and shalt believe in thine heart that God hath raised Him from the dead, thou shalt be saved. For with the heart man believeth unto righteousness; and with the mouth confession is made unto salvation" (Romans 10:9,10).

The life of confession is the life of full salvation. Indeed, the life of confession is the life of the only real salvation. When we confess Christ before men on earth, He acknowledges us before the Father in heaven. Then the Father gives us the Holy Spirit as the seal of our salvation.

It is not enough that we confess Christ just once, for example when we are confirmed, unite with the church, or come forward in a revival meeting. We should confess Christ constantly. We should not be ashamed of our Lord and King. In our home, church, work, and play, we should let others know where we stand. Of course, we should not parade our Christianity or our piety, but we should leave no one in doubt whether we belong to Christ. We should let it be seen that we honor Him as our Lord and King.

Backsliding

The failure to confess Christ is one of the most frequent causes of backsliding. Christians get into new relationships where they are not known as Christians and where they are tempted to conceal the fact. They yield to the temptation and soon find themselves drifting.

The more you make of Jesus Christ, the more He will make of you. It will save you from many a temptation if the fact is clear that you are one who acknowledges Christ as Lord in all things.

Chapter 3

ASSURANCE OF SALVATION

If one is to have the fullest measure of joy and power in Christian service, one must know that his sins are forgiven, that he is a child of God, and that he has eternal life. It is the believer's privilege to *know* he has eternal life. John says in 1 John 5:13, "These things have I written unto you that believe on the name of the Son of God; *that ye may know* that ye have eternal life, even unto you that believe on the name of the Son of God." John wrote this first epistle for the express purpose that anyone who believes on the name of the Son of God *will know* he has eternal life.

Eternal Life For His Children

There are those who tell us no one can know he has eternal life until he is dead and has been before the judgment seat of God. But God Himself tells us we may know. To deny the possibility of the believer's knowing he has eternal life is to say that the first epistle of John was written in vain, and it is to insult the Holy Spirit who is its real author.

Again Paul tells us in Acts 13:39, "By Him (that is by Christ) all that believe *are justified* from all things." So everyone who believes in Jesus can know that he is justified from all things. He knows it because the Word of God says so. John tells us in John 1:12, "But *as many as received Him* (that is Jesus Christ), to them gave He power to become the sons of God, even to them that believe on His name."

Here is a definite and unmistakable declaration that everyone who receives Jesus becomes a child of God. Therefore, every believer in Jesus may know that he is a child of God. He may know it on the surest of all grounds—the Word of God asserts that he is a child of God.

Faith In Fact Not Feeling

But how can any individual know he has eternal life? He can know it on the very best authority, that is through the testimony of God Himself as given in the Bible. The testimony of Scripture is the testimony of God. What the Scriptures say is absolutely true. What the Scriptures say, God says. Now in John 3:36 the Scriptures say, "He that believeth on the Son *hath* everlasting life." We know whether we believe on the Son or not. We know whether we have that real faith in Christ that leads us to receive Him. If we have this faith in Christ, we have God's own written testimony that we have eternal life, our sins are forgiven, and we are the children of God. We may feel forgiven, or

22

we may not feel forgiven, but that does not matter. It is not a question of what we feel but of what God says. God's Word is always to be believed.

Our own feelings are often to be doubted. There are many who doubt their sins are forgiven, who doubt they have everlasting life, who doubt they are saved. They can have doubts because they do not feel forgiven or feel that they have everlasting life or feel that they are saved. Not feeling forgiven is no reason to doubt.

Suppose you were sentenced to prison and your friends secured a pardon for you. The legal document announcing your pardon would be brought to you. You would read it and know you were pardoned because the legal document said so. But the news would be so good and so sudden that you would be dazed by it. You would not realize you were pardoned. Someone could come to you and say, "Are you pardoned?" What would you reply? You might say, "Yes, I am pardoned." Then he might ask, "Do you feel pardoned?" You may reply, "No, I do not feel pardoned. It is so sudden, it is so wonderful, I cannot comprehend it."

Then he would say to you, "But how can you know that you are pardoned if you do not feel it?" You would hold out the document and say, "This says so." The time would come, after you read the document over and over again and believed it, when you would not only know you were pardoned, but you would feel it.

The Bible is God's authoritative document declaring that everyone who believes in Jesus is justified. It declares that everyone who believes on the Son has everlasting life. It declares that everyone who receives Jesus is a child of God. If anyone asks you if your sins are all forgiven, reply, "Yes, I know they are because God says so." If anyone asks you if you know you are a child of God, reply, "Yes, I know I am a child of God because God says so." If they ask you if you have everlasting life, reply, "Yes, I know I have everlasting life because God says so."

God says, "Everyone which seeth the Son, and believeth on Him, may have everlasting life" (John 6:40). Then you can say, "I know I believe on the Son, and therefore I know I have eternal life—because God says so." You may not feel it yet but, if you keep meditating on God's statement and believe what God says, the time will come when you will feel it.

God Is Not A Liar

If one who believes on the Son of God doubts he has eternal life, he makes God a liar. "He that believeth on the Son of God hath the witness in himself. He that believeth not God hath made Him a liar; because he believeth not the record that God gave of His Son. And this is the record, that God hath given to us eternal life, and this life is in His Son. He that hath the Son hath life; and he that hath not the Son of God hath not life" (1 John 5:10-12). Anyone who does not believe God's testimony—that He has given us eternal life, His Son, and that he who has the Son has the life—makes

God a liar.

It is sometimes said, "It is presumptuous for anyone to say that he knows he is saved or to say he knows he has eternal life." But is it presumptuous to believe God? Is it not rather presumptuous not to believe God, to claim God is a liar? When you believe on the Son of God and yet doubt that you have eternal life, you make God a liar.

When Jesus said to the woman who was a sinner, "Thy sins are forgiven" (Luke 7:48), was it presumptuous for her to go out and say, "I know my sins are forgiven"? Would it not have been presumptuous for her to have doubted for a moment that her sins were all forgiven? Jesus said that they were forgiven. For her to doubt it would have been for her to give the lie to Jesus. Is it then any more presumptuous for the believer today to say, "My sins are all forgiven, I have eternal life," when God says in His written testimony to everyone who believes, "You are justified from all things" (Acts 13:39), "You have eternal life" (John 3:36; 1 John 5:13)?

Be very sure first of all that you really do believe on the name of the Son of God, that you really have received Jesus. If you are sure of this, then never doubt for a moment that your sins are all forgiven. Never doubt for a moment that you are a child of God. Never doubt for a moment that you have everlasting life.

Your Sins Are Forgiven

If Satan comes and whispers, "Your sins are not

forgiven," point Satan to the Word of God and say, "God says my sins are forgiven and I know they are." If Satan whispers, "Well, perhaps you don't believe on Him," then say, "Well if I never did before I will now." And then go out rejoicing, knowing your sins are forgiven, knowing you are a child of God, knowing you have everlasting life.

There are, without a doubt, many who say they know they have eternal life who really do not believe on the name of the Son of God. This is not true assurance. It has no sure foundation in the Word of God which does not lie. If we wish to get assurance of salvation, we must first become saved.

The reason many do not have the assurance they are saved is they are *not* saved. They need *salvation* before they need *assurance*. But if you have received Jesus in the way described in the first chapter, *you are saved*, you are a child of God, your sins are forgiven. Believe it. Know it. Rejoice in it.

Having settled the question, let it remain settled. Never doubt it. You may make mistakes; you may stumble; you may fall. Even if you do, if you have really received Jesus, you know that your sins are forgiven. You can rise from your fall and go forward in the glad assurance that there is nothing between you and God.

Chapter 4

RECEIVING THE HOLY SPIRIT

When the apostle Paul came to Ephesus, he found a small group of Christians. There was something about these disciples that struck Paul unfavorably. We are not told what it was. It may be that he did not find in them that overflowing joy one learns to expect in all Christians who have really entered into the fullness of blessing there is for them in Christ. It may be that Paul was troubled by the fact that there were so few of them. He may have thought that if these disciples were what they ought to be, there would certainly be more by this time.

The Holy Spirit Is Available

Whatever impressed Paul unfavorably, he went right to the root of the difficulty at once by asking them, "Have ye received the Holy Ghost since ye believed?" (Acts 19:2). It came out at once they had not received the Holy Spirit, that, in fact, they did not know the Holy Spirit was available to them.

Then Paul told them the Holy Spirit had been given. He also showed them what they had to do to receive the Holy Spirit. Before that gathering was over the Holy Spirit came upon them. From that day on there was a different state of affairs in Ephesus. A great revival began at once so that the whole city was shaken, "So mightily grew the Word of God and prevailed" (Acts 19:20).

Paul's question to these young disciples in Ephesus should be put to young disciples everywhere, "Have ye received the Holy Ghost?" *Receiving the Holy Spirit* is the great secret of joyfulness in our own hearts, victory over sin, power in prayer, and effective service.

The Spirit Dwells In Every Christian

Everyone who has truly received Jesus has the Holy Spirit dwelling in him in some sense. In many believers, though the Holy Spirit dwells within, He is back in some hidden sanctuary of their being, not a part of their consciousness. It is something quite different, something far better, to receive the Holy Spirit in the sense that Paul meant in his question. To receive the Holy Spirit in such a way that one knows without a doubt that he has received Him is to become conscious of the joy with which He fills our hearts. This joy is different from any joy we have ever known in the world. We can receive the Holy Spirit in such fullness that He rules our life and produces within us, in ever-increasing measure, the fruit of the Spirit. The fruit of the Spirit is love, joy, peace, long-

28

suffering, gentleness, goodness, faith, meekness, temperance.

Paul wanted all Christians to receive the Holy Spirit in such a sense that we are conscious of His drawing our hearts out in prayer in a way that is not of ourselves. He wanted us to receive the Holy Spirit in such a way that we are conscious of His help when we witness for Christ. We are conscious of His aid when we speak to others individually and try to lead them to accept Christ when we teach a Sunday school class, speak in public, or do any other work for the Master. Have you received the Holy Spirit? If you have not, this is how you may.

Steps For Holy Spirit Filling

1. First of all, in order to receive the Holy Spirit, one must acknowledge the death of Christ on the cross for us as the only and all-sufficient ground upon which God pardons all our sins.

2. In order to receive the Holy Spirit, we must put away every known sin. We must go to our heavenly Father and ask Him to search us through and through bringing to light anything in our outward life or inward life that is wrong in His sight. If He does bring anything to mind that is displeasing to Him, we should put it away, no matter how dear it is to us. There must be a complete renunciation of all sin in order to receive the Holy Spirit.

3. Third, in order to receive the Holy Spirit, we must openly confess Christ before the world. The Holy Spirit is not given to those who are trying to

be disciples in secret, but to those who obey Christ and publicly confess Him before the world. "Whosoever shall confess Me before men" (Luke 12:8).

4. Fourth, in order to receive the Holy Spirit, there must be absolute surrender of our lives to God. You must go to Him and say, "Heavenly Father, here I am. You have bought me with a price. I am Your property. I renounce all claim to do my own will, all claim to govern my own life, all claim to have my own way. I give myself up unreservedly to You—all I am and all I have. Send me where You want, use me as You like, do with me what You want—I am Yours."

If we hold anything back from God, no matter how small it may seem, that spoils everything. But if we surrender all to God, then God will give all He has to us. There are some who shrink from this absolute surrender to God, but absolute surrender to God is simply absolute surrender to infinite love. It is surrender to the Father—the Father whose love is not only wiser than any earthly father's, but more tender than any earthly mother's.

5. In order to receive the Holy Spirit there should be definite asking for the Holy Spirit. Our Lord Jesus says in Luke 11:13, "If ye then, being evil, know how to give good gifts unto your children: how much more shall your heavenly Father give the Holy Spirit to them that ask Him?" Just ask God to give you the Holy Spirit and expect Him to do it. He says He will.

6. Finally, in order to receive the Holy Spirit, there must be faith. Simply taking God at His Word. No matter how positive any promise of God's Word may be, we enjoy it personally only when we believe. Our Lord Jesus says, "What things soever ye desire, when ye pray, believe that ye receive them, and ye shall have them" (Mark 11:24).

When you pray for the Holy Spirit, you have prayed for something according to God's will. Therefore, you know that your prayer is heard and that you have what you asked of Him. "And this is the confidence we have in Him, that if we ask any thing according to His will, He heareth us: And if we know that He hear us, whatsoever we ask, we know that we have the petitions that we desired of Him" (1 John 5:14-15). You may feel no different, but do not look at your feelings but at God's promise. Believe the prayer is heard, believe that God has given you the Holy Spirit, and you will then have in actual experience what you have received in simple faith—on the bare promise of God's Word.

Give The Spirit Control

It is good to kneel down alone and look up to Jesus, putting into His hands anew the entire control of your life. Ask Him to take control of your thoughts, imaginations, affections, desires, ambitions, choices, purposes, words, and actions. In other words, ask Him to take control of everything. Then expect Him to do it. The whole secret of victory in the Christian life is letting the Holy Spirit, who dwells within you, have undisputed right of way in the entire conduct of your life.

Chapter 5

LOOKING TO JESUS

If we are to run with patience the race that is set before us, we must always keep looking to Jesus. "Wherefore seeing we also are compassed about with so great a cloud of witnesses let us lay aside every weight, and the sin which doth so easily beset us, and let us run with patience the race that is set before us, Looking to Jesus the author and finisher of our faith; who for the joy that was set before Him endured the cross, despising the shame, and is set down at the right hand of the throne of God. For consider Him that endured such contradiction of sinners against Himself, lest ye be wearied and faint in your minds" (Hebrews 12:1-3). One of the simplest, yet mightiest, secrets of abiding joy and victory is to *never lose sight of Jesus.*

Focus On Jesus Not Your Sins

First of all, *we must keep looking at Jesus as the reason for our acceptance before God.* Over and over again Satan will attempt to discourage us by recalling our sins and failures. He trys to convince us that we are neither children of God nor saved. If he succeeds in getting us to keep looking at and brooding over our sins, he will soon coax us to become discouraged. Discouragement means failure.

But if we keep looking at what God sees—the death of Jesus Christ in our place that completely atoned for every sin we ever committed—we will never be discouraged because of the greatness of our sins. We will see that, while our sins are very great, they have all been erased. Every time Satan brings up one of our sins, we will see that Jesus Christ has redeemed us from its curse by being made a curse in our place. "Christ hath redeemed us from the curse of the law, being made a curse for us: for it is written, Cursed is every one that hangeth on a tree" (Galatians 3:13).

We will see that "He hath made Him to be sin for us, who knew no sin; that we might be made the righteousness of God in Him" (2 Corinthians 5:21). In short, whenever Satan taunts us about our sin, we will know they have been washed away forever. "Who His own self bare our sins in His own body on the tree, that we, being dead to sins, should live unto righteousness: by whose stripes ye were healed" (1 Peter 2:24).

If you are troubled right now, about any sin you have ever committed, either past or present, just look at Jesus on the cross. Believe what God tells you about Him, that this sin which troubles you was laid upon Him (Isaiah 53:6). Thank God that the sin is all settled. Be full of gratitude to Jesus who bore it in your place, and do not worry about your sins anymore.

It is an act of base ingratitude toward God to brood over sins that He in His infinite love has cancelled. Keep looking at Christ on the cross and always walk in the sunlight of God's favor. This favor has been purchased for you at a high cost. Gratitude demands that you always believe in Jesus' gift and walk in the light of it.

Jesus Keeps Us Every Day

Secondly, *we must keep looking at Jesus as our risen Savior, who has all power in heaven and on earth and is able to keep us every day and every hour*. Are you tempted to do some wrong at this moment? If you are, remember that Jesus rose from the dead. Remember that at this moment He is living at the right hand of God in glory. Remember He has all power in heaven and on earth, and He can give you victory right now.

Believe what God tells you in His Word that Jesus has power to save you this moment "to the uttermost" (Hebrews 7:25). Believe He has power to give you victory over this sin that now attacks you. Ask Him to give you victory and expect Him to do it. In this way, by looking to the risen Christ for victory, you will have victory over sin every day, every hour, every minute. "Remember, that Jesus Christ was raised from the dead" (2 Timothy 2:8).

God called every one of us to a victorious life.

35

The secret of this victorious life is always looking to the risen Christ for victory. Through looking to Christ's sacrifice, we obtain pardon and enjoy peace. By looking to the risen Christ, we obtain present victory over the power of sin.

If you have lost sight of the risen Christ and have yielded to temptation, confess your sin and know that it is forgiven because God says so. "If we confess our sins, He is faithful and just to forgive us our sins, and to cleanse us from all unrighteousness" (1 John 1:9). Look to Jesus, the risen One, to give you victory now, then keep looking to Him.

Jesus Is Our Example

Third, *we must keep looking to Jesus as the One who we should follow in our daily conduct*. Our Lord Jesus says to us, His disciples today, as He said to His early disciples, "Follow Me" (Matthew 9:9). The whole secret of true Christian conduct can be summed up in these two words: "Follow Me." "He that saith he abideth in Him ought himself also to walk, *even as He walked*" (1 John 2:6).

One of the most common causes of failure in Christian life is found in the attempt to follow a good man whom we greatly admire. No man or woman, no matter how good, can be safely followed. If we follow any man or woman, we are bound to go astray. There has only been one absolutely perfect Man on this earth—the Man Christ Jesus. If we try to follow any other man, we are more sure to imitate his faults than his virtues. Look to Jesus and only Jesus as your guide.

If you are ever perplexed as to what to do, simply ask, "What would Jesus do?" Ask God through His Holy Spirit to show you what Jesus would do. Study your Bible to find out what Jesus did do and follow His example. Even though no one else seems to be following Jesus, be sure you follow Him.

Do not spend your time or thought criticizing others because they do not follow Jesus. See that you follow Him yourself. When you are wasting your time criticizing others for not following Jesus, Jesus is always saying to you, "What is that to thee; follow *thou* Me" (John 21:22). The question for you is not what following Jesus may involve for other people. The question is, what does following Jesus mean for you?

This is the life of a disciple—the life of simply following Jesus. Many perplexing questions will come to you, but the most perplexing question will soon become crystal clear if you determine with all your heart to follow Jesus in everything. Satan will always be ready to whisper to you, "Such and such a good man does it." But all you need to do is answer, "It does not matter to me what this or that man does." The only question should be, "What would Jesus do?"

There is wonderful freedom in this life of simply following Jesus. This path is straight and clear. But the path of the one who tries to shape his conduct by observing the conduct of others is full of twists, turns, and pitfalls. Keep looking at Jesus. Follow on with trust wherever He leads. "The path of the just is as the shining light, that shineth more and more unto the perfect day" (Proverbs 4:18). He is the light of the world. Anyone who follows Him will not walk in darkness, but will have the light of life all along the way (see John 8:12).

Chapter 6

CHURCH MEMBERSHIP

No Christian can have real success in the Christian life without the fellowship of other believers. The Church is a divine institution, built by Jesus Christ Himself. It is the one institution that endures. Other institutions come and go. They do their work for their day and disappear. But the Church will continue to the end. "The gates of hell shall not prevail against it" (Matthew 16:18). The Church is made up of men and women, imperfect men and women, consequently it is an imperfect institution. Nonetheless it is of divine origin, and God loves it. Every believer should realize that he belongs to it, openly take his place in it, and shoulder his responsibilities regarding it.

The Church consists of all believers who are united to Jesus Christ by a living faith in Him. In its outward organization today, it is divided into many sects and local congregations. In spite of these divisions, the Church is one. It has one Lord, Jesus Christ. It has one faith, faith in Him as Savior, divine Lord, and only King. All believe in one baptism, the baptism in one Spirit into one body. "For by one Spirit are we all baptized into one body, whether we be Jews or Gentiles, whether we be bond or free; and have been all made to drink into one Spirit" (1 Corinthians 12:13). "There is one body, and one Spirit, even as ye are called in one hope of your calling; One Lord, one faith, one baptism" (Ephesians 4:4,5).

Join A Body Of Believers

But each individual Christian needs the fellowship of individual fellow believers. The outward expression of this fellowship is membership in some organized body of believers. If we remain aloof from all organized churches, hoping to have a broader fellowship with all believers belonging to all churches, we deceive ourselves. We will miss the helpfulness that comes from intimate union with a local congregation.

I have known many well-meaning people who have neglected membership in any specific organization. I have never known a person to do this, whose spiritual life has not suffered. On the day of Pentecost the three thousand who were converted were baptized at once and were added to the Church. "They continued steadfastly in the apostles' doctrine and fellowship, in breaking of bread, and in prayers" (Acts 2:42). Their example is the one to follow. If you have really received Jesus Christ, as soon as possible find a group of people who have also received Him and unite yourself with them.

There Is No Perfect Church

In many communities there may be no choice of churches, because there is only one. In other communities, one will be faced with the question, "Which body of believers should I join?" Do not waste your time looking for a perfect church. There is no perfect church. A church in which you are the only member is the most imperfect church of all. I would rather belong to the most faulty Christian body of believers I ever knew than not belong to any church group at all.

The local churches in Paul's day were very imperfect institutions. Read the epistles to the Corinthians and see how imperfect the church in Corinth was. See how much evil was in it. Yet, Paul never dreamed of advising any believer in Corinth to get out of this imperfect church. He did tell them to come out of heathenism and to come out from fellowship with infidels. "Be ye not unequally yoked together with unbelievers: for what fellowship hath righteousness with unrighteousness? and what communion hath light with darkness? And what concord hath Christ with Belial? or what part hath he that believeth with an infidel? And what agreement hath the temple of God with idols? for ye are the temple of the living God; as God hath said, I will dwell in them and walk with them; and I will be their God, and they shall be My people. Wherefore come out from among them, and be ye separate, saith the Lord, and touch not the unclean thing; and I will receive you, And will be a Father unto you, and ye shall be my sons and daughters, saith the Lord Almighty" (2 Corinthians 6:14-18). He never advised coming out of the imperfect church in Corinth. Though he told the Corinthian church to separate from membership certain persons whose lives were wrong, he never advised anyone to leave the body because these people were not yet separated. "But now I have written unto you not to keep company, if any man that is called a brother be a fornicator, or covetous, or an idolator, or a railer, or a drunkard, or an extortioner; with such an one no not to eat" (1 Corinthians 5:11).

Guidelines For Finding A Church

Since you cannot find a perfect church, find the best church possible. Unite with a church where they believe in the Bible and where they preach the Bible. Avoid the churches where words, whether open or veiled, are spoken which have a tendency to undermine your faith in the Bible as a reliable revelation from God Himself. The Bible is the all-sufficient rule of faith and practice.

Unite with a church where there is a spirit of prayer, where the prayer meetings are well maintained. Unite with a church that has an active interest in the salvation of the lost, where young Christians are looked after and helped, where minister and people have a love for the poor and the destitute. Consider a church that regards its mission in this world to be the same as the mission of Christ, "to seek and to save that which was lost"

(Luke 19:10).

As to denominational differences, other things being equal, unite with that denomination whose ideas of doctrine, government, and ordinances are most closely related to your own. It is better to join a living church of another denomination than to unite with a dead church of your own. We live in a day when denominational differences are becoming less and less important. Often they have no practical value whatever. One can often feel more at home in a church of another denomination than in a church of his own denomination. The things that divide the denominations are insignificant compared with the great fundamental truths, purposes, and faith that unite them.

If you cannot find a church that agrees with the pattern set forth above, find a church that comes nearest to it. Go into that church and by prayer and work try to bring that church, as nearly as you can, to be what a church of Christ should be. Do not waste your strength in criticism against either the church or minister. Focus on what is good in the church and in the minister, and do your best to strengthen it. Keep a firm but unobtrusive distance from what is wrong while seeking to correct it.

Do not be discouraged if you cannot correct problems in a day, a week, a month, or a year. Patient love, prayer, and effort will show in time. Withdrawing by yourself, complaining, and grumbling will do no good. Grumbling will simply make you and the truths for which you stand repulsive.

Chapter 7

BIBLE STUDY

There is nothing more important for the development of a Christian's spiritual life than regular, systematic Bible study. It is as true in the spiritual life as in the physical life, that health depends on what we eat and how much we eat. "Man shall not live by bread alone" (Matthew 4:4). The soul's proper food is found in one book, the Bible.

Of course, a true minister of the gospel will feed us on the Word of God, but that is not enough. He feeds us only one or two days in the week, and we need to be fed every day. Furthermore, do not depend on being fed by others. We must learn to feed ourselves. If we study the Bible for ourselves as we should study it, we will be, in large measure, independent of human teachers. We will always be safe from spiritual harm, even if we are so unfortunate as to have a man who is ignorant of God's truth for our minister. We live in a day in which false doctrine is everywhere, and the only Christian who is safe from being led into error is the one who studies his Bible for himself, daily.

The Word Keeps Us Safe

The apostle Paul warned the elders of the church in Ephesus that the time was soon coming when vicious wolves would join them and not spare the flock. They would speak perverse things of their own creation trying to draw disciples away from Jesus. But Paul told them how to be safe even in such perilous times as these. He said, "I commend you to God, and to the Word of His grace, which is able to build you up, and to give you an inheritance among all them which are sanctified" (Acts 20:32).

Through meditation on the Word of God's grace, they would be safe even in the midst of flourishing error on the part of leaders in the church. "For I know this, that after my departing shall grievous wolves enter in among you, not sparing the flock. Also of your own selves shall men arise, speaking perverse things, to draw away disciples after them. Therefore watch, and remember, that by the space of three years I ceased not to warn every one night and day with tears" (Acts 20:29-31).

Writing later to the bishop of the church in Ephesus, Paul said, "But evil men and seducers shall wax worse and worse, deceiving, and being deceived" (2 Timothy 3:13). But he goes on to tell Timothy how he and his fellow believers could remain safe even in the times of increasing peril that were coming. This could be done through the study of the Holy Scriptures, which gives readers wisdom, drawing them to salvation. "But continue thou in the things which thou hast learned and hast been assured of, knowing of whom thou hast learned them; And that from a child thou hast known the holy scriptures, which are able to make thee wise unto salvation through faith which is in Christ Jesus" (2 Timothy 3:14,15).

Bible Study Brings Success

"All Scripture," he adds, "is given by inspiration of God, and is profitable for doctrine, for reproof, for correction, for instruction in righteousness: That the man of God may be perfect, thoroughly furnished unto all good works" (2 Timothy 3:16). Through the study of the Bible, one will be sound in doctrine and led to see his sins and to put them away. He will find discipline in the righteous life and be equipped for all good works. Our spiritual health, growth, strength, victory over sin, soundness in doctrine, joy, and peace in Christ come from study of God's Word. Cleansing from inward and outward sin and fitness for service all depend on daily study of the Bible.

The one who neglects his Bible is bound to be a failure in the Christian life. The one who studies his Bible in the right spirit and by a constant method is bound to make a success of the Christian life. This brings us face to face with the question, "What is the right way to study the Bible?"

How To Study Your Bible

First of all, we should *study it daily*. "These were more noble than those in Thessalonica, in that they received the word with all readiness of mind, and searched the scriptures daily, whether those things were so" (Acts 17:11). This is of prime importance. No matter how solid the methods of Bible study, how much time one may put into Bible study now and then, the best results can only be secured when one never lets a single day go by without earnest Bible study. This is the only safe course. Any day that is allowed to pass without faithful Bible study is a day which opens our hearts and lives to error and sin. The writer has been a Christian for more than a quarter of a century, and yet today he would not dare allow even a single day to pass without listening to God's voice as He speaks through the pages of His Book.

It is with this responsibility that many fall away. They grow careless and let a day pass, or even several days, without spending time alone with God or letting Him speak to them through His Word. Mr. Moody once wisely said, "In prayer we talk to God. In Bible study, God talks to us, and we had better let God do most of the talking."

A regular time should be set aside each day for Bible study. I do not think it is wise, as a rule, to say that we will study so many chapters a day, because that leads to undue haste, skimming, and thoughtlessness. But it is good to set apart a certain length of time each day for Bible study. Some can give more time to Bible study than others, but no one should devote less than fifteen minutes a day.

I set a short time span so that no one will be discouraged in the beginning. If a young Christian planned to spend an hour or two a day in Bible study, there is a strong probability that he would not keep the resolution and would become discouraged. Nevertheless, I know of many very busy people who have taken the first hour of every day for years for Bible study. Some have even given two hours a day.

The late Earl Cairns, Lord Chancellor of England, was one of the busiest men of his day. Lady Cairns told me that no matter how late at night he reached home, he always woke up at the same early hour for prayer and Bible study. She said, "We would sometimes get home from Parliament at two o'clock in the morning, but Lord Cairns would always arise at the same early hour to pray and study the Bible." Lord Cairns is reported as saying, "If I have had any success in life, I attribute it to the habit of giving the first two hours of each day to Bible study and prayer."

It is important that one *choose the right time for this study*. Whenever possible, the best time for study is immediately after waking up in the morning. The worst time is the last thing at night. Of course, it is good to spend a little time just before we go to bed reading the Bible so that God's voice will be the last voice we hear. The bulk of our Bible study should be done when our minds are clearest and strongest. Whatever time is set apart for Bible study should be kept sacredly for that purpose.

We should *study the Bible systematically*. A lot of time is frittered away in random study of the Bible. The same amount of time put into systematic study would yield far greater results. Have a definite place where you study and have a definite plan of study. A good way for a young Christian to begin the study of the Bible is to read the gospel of John. When you have read it through once, read it again until you have gone over the gospel five times. Then read the gospel of Luke five times in the same way. Then read the Acts of the Apostles five times. Then read the following epistles five times each: 1 Thessalonians, 1 John, Romans, and Ephesians.

By this time you will be ready to take up a more thorough method of Bible study. A profitable method is to begin at Genesis and *read the Bible through chapter by chapter*. Read each chapter through several times and then answer the following questions on each chapter:

1) What is the main subject of the chapter? State the principal contents of the chapter in a single phrase or sentence.

2) What is the truth most clearly taught and most emphasized in the chapter?

3) What is the best lesson?

4) What is the best verse?

5) Who are the principal people mentioned?

6) What does the chapter teach about Jesus

Christ?

Go through the entire Bible in this way.

Another and more thorough method of Bible study will yield excellent results when applied to some of the more important chapters of the Bible. However, it cannot be applied to every chapter in the Bible. It is as follows:

1) Read the chapter for today's study five times, reading it out loud at least once. Each new reading will bring out a new point.

2) Divide the chapter into its natural divisions, and find headings that describe the contents of each division. For example, suppose the chapter studied is 1 John 5. You might divide it this way: first division, verses 1-3, *The Believer's Noble Parentage;* second division, verses 4-5, *The Believer's Glorious Victory;* third division, verses 6-10, *The Believer's Sure Ground of Faith.* Continue through each division this way.

3) Note the important differences between the King James Version and the Revised Standard Version.

4) Write down the most important facts of the chapter in their proper order.

5) Make a note of the people mentioned in the chapter and any light thrown on their character.

6) Note the principal lessons of the chapter. It is helpful to classify these. For instance, lessons about God, lessons about Christ, lessons about the Holy Spirit, etc.

7) Find the central truth of the chapter.

8) Find the key verse of the chapter if there is

one.

9) Find the best verse in the chapter. Mark it and memorize it.

10) Write down any new truth you have learned from the chapter.

11) Write down any truth you already know that has come to you with new power.

12) Write down what definite thing you have resolved to do as a result of studying this chapter. A beneficial order of study for you might be all of the chapters in Matthew, Mark, Luke, John, and Acts; the first eight chapters of Romans; 1 Corinthians 12, 13, and 15; the first six chapters of 2 Corinthians; then all of the chapters in Galatians, Ephesians, Philippians, 1 Thessalonians, and 1 John. Sometimes you can refresh your study by alternating methods.

Another profitable method of Bible study is *the topical method.* This was D. L. Moody's favorite method. Take such topics as: the Holy Spirit, prayer, the blood of Christ, sin, judgment, grace, justification, the new birth, sanctification, faith, repentance, the character of Christ, the resurrection of Christ, the ascension of Christ, the second coming of Christ, assurance, love of God, love (to God, to Christ, to Christians, to all men), heaven, hell. Get a Bible concordance and study each one of these topics.

We should *study the Bible comprehensively*— the whole Bible. Many Bible readers make the mistake of confining all their reading to certain portions of the Bible that they enjoy. This way they get no knowledge of the Bible as a whole. They miss altogether many of the most important phases of Bible truth. Go through the Bible again and again—a certain portion each day from the Old Testament and a portion from the New Testament. Read carefully at least one Psalm every day.

It is also beneficial to read a whole book of the Bible through at a single sitting. This lets you see the whole picture. Of course, a few books of the Bible would take one or two hours. But most books can be read in a few minutes. The shorter books of the Bible should be read through again and again at a single sitting.

Study the Bible attentively. Do not hurry. One of the worst faults in Bible study is haste. We only benefit from Bible study by learning its truth. It has no magic power. It is better to read one verse attentively than to read a dozen chapters thoughtlessly. Sometimes you will read a verse that grabs you. Don't hurry on. Stop and think about that verse.

As you read, mark in your Bible what impresses you most. One does not need an elaborate marking system, simply highlight what impresses you. Think about what you mark. God affirms that the man who meditates on God's law day and night is blessed. "But his delight is in the law of the Lord; and in His law doth he meditate day and night" (Psalm 1:2).

It is wonderful how a verse of Scripture will open one's mind to its exact meaning. Memorize the passages that impress you most. "Thy word have I hid in mine heart, that I might not sin against Thee" (Psalm 119:11). When you memorize a passage of Scripture, memorize its location as well as the words. A busy but spiritually-minded man who was hurrying to catch a train once said to me, "Tell me in a word how to study my Bible." I replied, "Thoughtfully."

Study your Bible comparatively. In other words, compare Scripture with Scripture. The best commentary on the Bible is the Bible itself. Wherever you find a difficult passage in the Bible, there is always another passage that explains its meaning. The best book to use in this comparison is *The Treasury of Scripture Knowledge.* This book gives a large number of references on every verse in the Bible. You may want to take a particular book of the Bible and go through that book verse by verse. Look up and study every reference given in *The Treasury of Scripture Knowledge* dealing with that book. This is a very fruitful method of Bible study. You will also gain by studying the Bible by chapters and looking up the references on the more important verses in each chapter. One will gain a better understanding of passages of Scripture by looking up the references given in *The Treasury of Scripture Knowledge.*

Study your Bible and believe it. The apostle Paul, in writing to the Christians in Thessalonica, said, "For this cause also thank we God without ceasing, because, when ye received the word of God which ye heard of us, ye received it not as the word of men, but as it is in truth, the word of God, which effectually worketh also in you that believe" (1 Thessalonians 2:13). Happy is the one who receives the Word of God as these believers in Thessalonica received it, as the Word of God. In such a person it is especially effective. The Bible is the Word of God, and we get the most out of any book by acknowledging it for what it really is.

It is often said that we should study the Bible just as we study any other book. That principle contains a truth, but it also contains a great error. The Bible, like other books, has the same laws of grammatical and literary construction. But the Bible is a unique book. It is what no other book is, the Word of God. This can be easily proven to any impartial man. The Bible should be studied, then, specifically as the Word of God. This involves five things.

It involves a greater eagerness and more careful, candid study to find out exactly what the Bible teaches. It is important to know the mind of man. It is absolutely essential to know the mind of God. The place to discover the mind of God is the Bible because it is here that God reveals His mind.

It requires a prompt and unquestioning acceptance of, and submission to, its teachings when definitely ascertained. These teachings may appear unreasonable or impossible. Nevertheless, we should accept them. If this book is the Word of God, it is foolish to submit its teachings to the criticism of our finite reasoning.

A little boy who discredits his wise father's statements simply because to his infant mind they appear unreasonable is not thinking wisely but foolishly. Even the greatest of human thinkers is only an infant compared with God. To discredit God's statements found in His Word because they appear unreasonable to our infantile minds shows our shallow thinking. When we are once satisfied that the Bible is the Word of God, its clear teachings must be the end of all controversy and discussion for us.

Correct Bible study includes absolute reliance on all its promises in all their length, breadth, depth, and height. The one who studies the Bible as the Word of God will say of any promise, no matter how vast and beyond belief it appears, "God who cannot lie has promised this, so I will claim it for myself."

Mark the promise you claim. Each day look for some new promise from your infinite Father. He has put "His riches in glory" at your disposal (Philippians 4:19). I know of no better way to grow rich spiritually than to search daily for promises; and when you find them, take them for yourself.

You must also study God's Word in obedience. "Be ye doers of the Word and not hearers only, deceiving your own selves" (James 1:22). Nothing goes farther to help one understand the Bible than resolving to obey it. Jesus said, "If any man will do His will, he shall know of the doctrine" (John 7:17). The surrendered will means a clear eye. If our eye is single (that is, our will is absolutely surrendered to God), our whole body will be full of light. But if our eye is evil (that is, if we are trying to serve two masters and are not absolutely surrendered to one Master, God), our whole body will be full of darkness. "The light of the body is the eye: if therefore thine eye be single, thy whole body shall be full of light. But if thine eye be evil, thy whole body shall be full of darkness. If therefore the light that is in thee be darkness, how great is that darkness! No man can serve two masters: for either he will hate the one, and love the other; or else he will hold to the one, and despise the other. Ye cannot serve God and mammon" (Matthew 6:22-24). Many passages that look obscure to you now would become as clear as day if you were willing to obey everything the Bible teaches.

Blessing Comes Through Obedience

Each commandment discovered in the Bible that is really intended as a commandment to us should be obeyed instantly. It is remarkable how soon one loses his thirst for the Bible and how soon the mind becomes obscured to its teachings when we disobey the Bible at any point. I have often known people who loved their Bibles, were useful in God's service, and had clear views of the truth. They then came to a command in the Bible they were unwilling to obey. Some sacrifice was demanded which they were unwilling to make. As a result, their love for the Bible rapidly waned, their faith in the Bible weakened, and soon they drifted farther and farther away from clear views of the truth.

Nothing clears the mind like obedience; nothing darkens the mind like disobedience. To obey a truth you see prepares you to see other truths. To disobey a truth you see darkens your mind to all truths.

Cultivate prompt, exact, unquestioning, joyous obedience to every command that clearly applies to you. Be on the lookout for new orders from your King. Blessing lies in the direction of obedience to them. God's commands are guideposts that mark the road to present success and to eternal glory.

Personal Companionship With God

Studying the Bible as the Word of God involves studying it *as His own voice speaking directly to you*. When you open the Bible to study, realize that you have come into the very presence of God and that He is going to speak to you. Realize that it is God who is talking to you as if you were looking at Him face to face. Say to yourself, "God is now going to speak to me." Nothing gives more freshness and gladness to Bible study than the realization that, as you read, God is actually talking to you.

Bible study then becomes personal companionship with God Himself. What a wonderful privilege Mary had one day, sitting at the feet of Jesus and listening to His voice. If we will study the Bible as the Word of God and as if we were in God's presence, then we will enjoy the privilege of sitting at the feet of Jesus and having Him talk to us every day.

This approach makes what would otherwise be a mere mechanical performance of a duty become a wonderfully joyous privilege. One can say as he opens the Bible, "Now, God my Father is going to speak to me." Reading the Bible on our knees helps us to realize we are in God's presence. The Bible became in some measure a new book to me when I took to reading it on my knees.

Study the Bible prayerfully. God, the author of the Bible, is willing to act as interpreter of it. He does so when you ask Him. The one who prays the psalmist's prayer with sincerity and faith, "Open Thou mine eyes, that I may behold wondrous things out of Thy law" (Psalm 119:18), will have his eyes opened to new beauties and wonders in the Word.

Be very definite about this. Each time you open the Bible for study, even though it is only for a few minutes, ask God to give you an open and discerning eye. Expect Him to do it. Every time you come to a difficult passage in the Bible, lay it before God, ask for an explanation, and expect it.

The Holy Spirit As Teacher

How often we think as we puzzle over hard passages, "Oh, if I only had some great Bible teacher here to explain this to me!" God is always present. He understands the Bible better than any human teacher. Take your difficulty to Him and ask Him to explain it. Jesus said, "When He the Spirit of truth is come, He will guide you into all the truth" (John 16:13). It is the privilege of the humblest believer in Christ to have the Holy Spirit for his guide in his study of the Word.

I have known many very humble people, people with almost no education, who got more out of their Bible study than many great theological teachers. This happened because they learned it was their privilege to have the Holy Spirit for their Bible study teacher. Commentaries on the Bible are usually valuable. But one will learn more from the Bible by having the Holy Spirit for his teacher than from all the commentaries ever published.

Use spare time for Bible study. Time is lost in almost every man's life while waiting for meals, riding planes, going from place to place, and so forth. Carry a pocket Bible with you and use these golden moments to listen to the voice of God.

Store Scripture in your mind and heart. It will keep you from sin (see Psalm 119:11) and false doctrine. (See Acts 20:29,30,32; and 2 Timothy 3:13-15.) "And Thy word was unto me the joy and rejoicing of mine heart" (Jeremiah 15:16). "For He will speak peace unto His people" (Psalm 85:8). It will give you victory over the evil one (see 1 John 2:14), and it will give you power in prayer. "If ye abide in Me and My words abide in you, ye shall ask what ye will, and it shall be done unto you" (John 15:7). The Word will make you wiser than the aged and your enemies. "Thou through Thy commandments hast made me wiser than mine enemies: for they are ever with me. I understand more than the ancients, because I keep Thy precepts. The entrance of Thy words giveth light; it giveth understanding unto the simple" (Psalm 119:98,100,130). It will make you "thoroughly furnished unto all good works"(2 Timothy 3:17). Try it.

Do not memorize at random but memorize Scripture in a connected way. Memorize texts on various subjects. Memorize by chapter and verse so that you will know where to put your finger on the text if anyone disputes it. You should have a good Bible for your study.

Chapter 8

DIFFICULTIES IN THE BIBLE

Sooner or later every young Christian comes across passages in the Bible which are hard to understand and difficult to believe. To many young Christians, these perplexities become a serious hindrance in the development of their Christian life. For days, weeks, and months, faith suffers a partial or total eclipse. At this point wise counsel is needed. We have no desire to conceal the fact that these difficulties exist. We desire instead to frankly face and consider them. What should we do concerning these paradoxes that every thoughtful student of the Bible will sooner or later encounter?

Expect Difficulties

The first thing we have to say about these difficulties is that, from the very nature of the situation, difficulties are to be expected. Some people are surprised and staggered because there are difficulties in the Bible. I would be more surprised and staggered if there were not. What is the Bible?

It is a revelation of the mind, will, character, and being of the infinitely great, perfectly wise, and absolutely holy God.

To whom is this revelation made? To men and women like you and me—finite beings. It comes to men who are imperfect in intellectual development, in knowledge, in character, and, consequently, in spiritual discernment.

Because of our weakness, there must be difficulties in such a revelation. When the finite tries to understand the infinite there is bound to be difficulty. When the ignorant contemplate the speech of one perfect in knowledge there will be many things which are hard to understand. Some things will also appear absurd to immature and inaccurate minds. When sinful beings listen to the demands of the absolutely holy being, they are bound to be staggered at some of His demands. When they consider His works, they are bound to be staggered. These will necessarily appear too severe, stern, and harsh.

It is plain that there must be difficulties for us in such a revelation as the Bible is proven to be. If someone were to hand me a book that was as simple as the multiplication table and say, "This is the Word of God, in which He has revealed His whole will and wisdom," I would shake my head and say, "I cannot believe it. That is too easy to be a perfect revelation of infinite wisdom." There must be in any complete revelation of God's mind, will, character, and being, things which are difficult for a beginner to understand. Even the wisest and best of us are only beginners.

The Bible Is God's Revelation

The second thing about these difficulties is that a difficulty in a doctrine, or a grave objection to a doctrine, does not in any way prove the doctrine to be untrue. Many thoughtless people imagine it does. If they come across some difficulty in believing the divine origin and absolute inerrancy and infallibility of the Bible, they immediately conclude that the doctrine is disproved. That is very illogical.

Stop a moment and think. Be reasonable and fair. There is scarcely a doctrine in modern science that has not had some great difficulty gaining acceptance. When the Copernican theory, now so universally accepted, was first proclaimed, it encountered a very serious dilemma. If this theory were true, the planet Venus had to have phases like the moon. But no phases could be discovered using the best telescope then in existence. The positive argument for the theory was so strong, however, that it was accepted in spite of this apparently unanswerable objection. When a more powerful telescope was made, it was discovered that Venus had phases after all.

The whole problem arose, as all those in the Bible arise, from man's ignorance of some of the facts in the case. According to the common sense logic recognized in many departments of science, if the positive proof of a theory is conclusive, it is believed by rational men in spite of any number of discrepancies in minor details. The positive proof that the Bible is the Word of God is absolutely conclusive: it is an absolutely trustworthy revelation from God Himself of Himself, His purposes and His will, of man's duty and destiny, of spiritual and eternal realities.

Therefore, every rational man and woman must believe it despite minor discrepancies. He is a shallow thinker who gives up a well-attested truth because there are some facts which he cannot reconcile with that truth. It is a very shallow Bible scholar who gives up the divine origin and inerrancy of the Bible because there are some supposed facts that he cannot reconcile with that doctrine.

The Bible Is Logical And Unified

There are many more difficulties in a doctrine that believes the Bible to be of human origin and hence fallible, than the doctrine that the Bible is of divine origin, hence altogether trustworthy. A man may bring you some apparent error and say, "How do you explain this if the Bible is the Word of God?" Perhaps you may not be able to answer him satisfactorily.

Then he thinks he has you, but not at all. Turn to him and ask him, "How do you account for the fulfilled prophecies of the Bible, if it is of human origin? How do you account for the marvelous unity of the Bible? How do you account for its inexhaustible depth? How do you account for its unique power in lifting men up to God? How do you account for the history of the book, its victory over all men's attacks, etc."

For every insignificant objection he can bring to your view, you can bring many deeply significant objections to his view. No impartial man will have any difficulty in deciding between the two views. The discrepancies that must confront one who denies the Bible is of divine origin and authority are far more numerous than those that confront people who do believe it is of divine origin.

We Do Not Know Everything

Do not think that because you cannot solve a difficulty you cannot prove that the difficulty cannot be solved. The fact that you cannot answer an objection does not prove at all that it cannot be answered. It is strange how often we overlook this very evident fact. There are many who, when they see something in the Bible that does not conform to their truth, give it little thought and promptly jump to the conclusion that a solution is impossible. They then throw away their faith in the reliability of the Bible and its divine origin. A little more modesty in beings so limited in knowledge, as we all are, would have led them to say, "Though I see no possible solution to this difficulty, someone a little wiser than I might easily find one."

Oh! If we would only bear in mind that we do not know everything and that there are a great many things that we cannot solve now but could easily solve if we only knew a little more. Above all, we should never forget that there may be a very easy solution through infinite wisdom which to our finite wisdom—or ignorance—appears absolutely insoluble.

What would we think of a beginner in algebra who, having tried without success for half an hour to solve a difficult problem, declared that there was no possible solution to the problem because he could not find one? A man with a lot of experience and ability once left his work and came a long distance to see me. He discovered what seemed to him to be a flat contradiction in the Bible. It defied all attempts at reconciliation. But in a few moments he saw a very simple and satisfactory solution to the difficulty.

A Beautiful And Wondrous Book

The seeming defects in the book are exceedingly insignificant when compared with its many, marvelous wonders. It certainly reveals great perversity of both mind and heart that men spend so much time focusing on the insignificant points that they consider defects in the Bible. How sad it is that they never recognize the incomparable beauties and wonders that adorn almost every page.

What would we think of any man who, in studying some great masterpiece of art, concentrated his entire attention on what looked to him like a flyspeck in the corner. A large proportion of what is vaunted as "critical study of the Bible" is a laborious and scholarly investigation of supposed flyspecks and an entire neglect of the countless glories of the book.

Are You A Superficial Reader?

The puzzles and paradoxes in the Bible have far more weight with superficial readers than with students who read it in depth. Take a man who is totally ignorant of the real contents and meaning of the Bible and devotes his whole strength to discovering apparent inconsistencies in it. To such superficial Bible students these difficulties seem to have immense importance; but to the one who has learned to meditate on the Word of God day and night, they have little weight.

That mighty man of God, George Mueller, who carefully studied the Bible from beginning to end more than a hundred times, was not disturbed by any discrepancies he encountered. His example can encourage the student who is reading it through carefully for the first or second time and finds many things that perplex him.

The difficulties in the Bible rapidly disappear upon careful and prayerful study. There are many things in the Bible that once puzzled us that have been perfectly cleared up and no longer present any difficulty at all! Is it not reasonable to suppose that the difficulties that still remain will also disappear on further study?

Profitable Approach To Discrepancies

How shall we deal with the difficulties which we do find in the Bible?

First of all, *honestly.* Whenever you find a difficulty in the Bible, frankly acknowledge it. If you cannot give a good, honest explanation, do not attempt as yet, to give any at all.

Humbly. Recognize the limitations of your own mind and knowledge, and do not imagine there is no solution just because you have not found one. There is, in all probability, a very simple solution. You will find it some day.

With determination. Make up your mind that you will find the solution, if possible, through necessary study and hard thinking. The difficulties in the Bible are your heavenly Father's challenge to you to set your brains to work.

Fearlessly. Do not be frightened when you find a difficulty, no matter how unanswerable it appears at first glance. Thousands have found such before you. They were seen hundreds of years ago and still the Bible stands. You are not likely to discover any difficulty that was not discovered and probably settled long before you were born, though you do not know just where to lay your hand on the solution.

The Bible, which has stood eighteen centuries of rigid examination and constant, intense assault, will not fail because of any discoveries you make or any attacks of modern infidels. All modern attacks on the Bible simply revamp old objections which have been disposed of a hundred times in the past. These old objections will prove no more effective in their new clothes than they did in the cast-off garments of the past.

Patiently. Do not be discouraged because you do not solve every problem in a day. If some difficulty defies your best effort, lay it aside for awhile. Very likely when you come back to it, it will have disappeared and you will wonder how you were ever perplexed by it. The writer often has to smile today when he remembers how he was perplexed in the past over questions which are now clear as day.

Scripturally. If you find a difficulty in one part of the Bible, look for other Scriptures to throw light on it and dissolve it. Nothing explains Scripture like Scripture. Never let apparently obscure passages of Scripture darken the light that comes from clear passages. Rather let the light that comes from the clear passage illuminate the darkness that seems to surround the obscure passage.

Prayerfully. It is wonderful how difficulties dissolve when one looks at them on his knees. One great reason some modern scholars have learned to be destructive critics is that they have forgotten how to pray.

Chapter 9

PRAYER

The one who wishes to succeed in the Christian life must lead a life of prayer. Much of the failure in Christian living today, and in Christian work, results from neglect of prayer. Very few Christians spend as much time in prayer as they should. The apostle James told believers in his day that the secret behind the poverty and powerlessness of their lives and service was neglect of prayer. "Ye have not," says God through the apostle James, "because ye ask not" (James 4:2). So it is today. "Why is it," many a Christian is asking, "that I make such poor headway in my Christian life? Why do I have so little victory over sin? Why do I accomplish so little by my effort?" God answers, "Ye have not because ye ask not."

Decide On A Life Of Prayer

It is easy enough to lead a life of prayer if one only decides to live it. Set apart some time each day for prayer. The habit of David and Daniel is a good one, three times a day. "Evening, and morning, and at noon," says David, "will I pray, and cry aloud: and He shall hear my voice" (Psalm 55:17). Of Daniel we read, "Now when Daniel knew that the writing was signed, he went into his house; and his windows being open in his chamber toward Jerusalem, he kneeled upon his knees three times a day, and prayed, and gave thanks before his God, as he did aforetime" (Daniel 6:10).

Of course, one can pray while walking down the street, riding in the car, or sitting at his desk. And one should learn to lift his heart to God right in the busiest moments of his life. But we also need set times of prayer, times when we go alone with God and talk to our Father in the secret place. "But thou, when thou prayest, enter into thy closet, and when thou hast shut thy door, pray to thy Father which is in secret; and thy Father which seeth in secret shall reward thee openly" (Matthew 6:6). God is in the secret place. He will meet with us there and listen to our petitions.

Prayer is a wonderful privilege. It is an audience with the King. It is talking to our Father. How strange it is that people would ask the question, "How much time should I spend in prayer?" When a person is summoned to an audience with his king, he never asks, "How much time must I spend with the king?" His question is rather, "How much time will the king give me?" Any true child of God, who realizes that prayer is an audience with the King of Kings, will never ask, "How much time must I spend in prayer?" Instead, he will ask, "How much time may I spend in prayer considering other duties and privileges?"

Prepare With Prayer

Begin the day with thanksgiving and prayer. Offer thanksgiving for the definite mercies of the past and prayer for the definite needs of the present day. Think of the temptations that you are likely to meet during the day. Ask God to show you these temptations and ask for strength from God for victory over them before they come. Many fail in the battle because they wait until the hour of battle to ask for aid. Others succeed because they have gained victory on their knees long before the battle arrived.

Jesus conquered the awful battles of Pilate's judgment hall and the cross because He prayed the previous night. He anticipated the battle the night before and gained the victory through prayer. He told His disciples to do the same. He instructed them, "Pray that ye enter not into temptation" (Luke 22:40), but they slept when they should have prayed. And when the hour of temptation came, they fell. Anticipate your battles, fight them on your knees before temptation comes, and you will always have victory. At the very start of the day, secure counsel and strength from God Himself for the duties of the day.

Prayer Saves Time

Never let the rush of business crowd out prayer. The more work that must be accomplished in any day, the more time must be spent in prayer and preparation for that work. You will not lose time by praying, you will save time. Prayer is the greatest time-saver known to man. The more work crowds you, the more you must take time for prayer.

Stop in the middle of the bustle and temptation of the day for thanksgiving and prayer. A few minutes spent alone with God at noon will go far to keep you calm despite the worries and anxieties of modern life.

Close the day with thanksgiving and prayer. Review all the blessings of the day and thank God in detail for them. Nothing further increases faith in God and His Word than a calm review at the close of each day of what God has done for you that day. Nothing goes further toward bringing new and larger blessings from God than intelligent thanksgiving for blessings already granted.

Close Your Day With A Clean Slate

As the last thing you do each day, ask God to show you anything that has been displeasing in His sight. Then wait quietly before Him and give God an opportunity to speak to you. Listen. Do not be in a hurry. If God shows you anything in the day that has been displeasing in His sight, confess it fully and frankly as to a holy and loving Father. Believe that God forgives it all, because He says He does. "If we confess our sins, He is faithful and just to forgive us our sins, and to cleanse us from all unrighteousness" (1 John 1:9).

Thus, at the close of each day, all your accounts with God will be settled. You can sleep in the joyful awareness that there is not a cloud between you and God. You can rise the next day to begin life anew with a clean balance sheet.

Do this and you can never backslide for more than twenty-four hours. Indeed, you will not backslide at all. It is very hard to straighten out accounts in business that have been allowed to become disordered over a prolonged period. No bank ever closes its business day until its balance sheet is absolutely correct. No Christian should close a single day until his accounts with God for that day have been perfectly adjusted.

Prayer For Specific Blessings

There should be special prayer in special temptation—when we see the temptation approaching. If you possibly can, immediately find a place to be alone somewhere with God, then fight your battle out. Keep looking to God. "Pray without ceasing" (1 Thessalonians 5:17). It is not necessary to always be on your knees, but the heart should be on its knees all the time. We should often be on our knees, or our faces literally.

This prayer life is a joyous life, free from worry and care. "Be careful for nothing; but in every thing by prayer and supplication with thanksgiving let your requests be made known unto God. And the peace of God, which passeth all understanding shall keep your hearts and minds through Christ Jesus" (Philippians 4:6,7).

77

There are three things for which one who desires to succeed in the Christian life must especially pray. *Wisdom.* "If any of you lack wisdom, (and we all do) let him ask of God" (James 1:5). *Strength.* "But they that wait upon the Lord shall renew their strength" (Isaiah 40:31). *The Holy Spirit.* "Your heavenly Father (shall) give the Holy Spirit to them that ask Him" (Luke 11:13).

Even if you have received the Holy Spirit, you should constantly pray for a new blessing of the Holy Spirit and definitely expect to receive it. We need to be in contact with the Spirit, ready for every new emergency of Christian life and Christian service. The apostle Peter was baptized and filled with the Holy Spirit on Pentecost. "And when the day of Pentecost was fully come, they were all with one accord in one place. And suddenly there came a sound from heaven as of a rushing mighty wind, and it filled all the house where they were sitting. And there appeared unto them cloven tongues like as of fire, and it sat upon each of them. And they were all filled with the Holy Ghost, and began to speak with other tongues, as the Spirit gave them utterance" (Acts 2:1-4). After his baptism, the Holy Spirit continued to work through Peter as recorded in Acts 4:8 and Acts 4:31. "Then Peter, filled with the Holy Ghost said unto them, Ye rulers of the people. . . .And when they had prayed, the place was shaken where they were assembled together; and they were all filled with the Holy Ghost and they spake the Word of God with boldness."

There are many Christians in the world who had a very definite baptism of the Holy Spirit. They experienced great joy and were wonderfully used. But many have tried ever since to continue with only the power of that baptism received years ago. Today their lives are comparatively joyless and powerless. We constantly need to obtain new supplies of oil for our lamps. We secure these new supplies of oil by asking for them.

Do Not Neglect Fellowship

It is not enough that we have our times of secret prayer alone with God. We also need fellowship with others in prayer. If there is a prayer meeting in your church, attend it regularly. Attend it for your own sake and for the sake of the church. If it is a prayer meeting only in name and not in fact, use your influence quietly and constantly (not obstrusively) to make it a real prayer meeting. Attend the prayer meeting regularly for that purpose. Refuse all social engagements for that night.

A major-general in the United States Army once took command of the forces in a new district. A reception was arranged for him on a certain night of the week. When he was informed of this public reception, he replied that he could not attend since it was the evening of his prayer meeting. Everything had to take second place on that night to his prayer meeting. That general proved he was a man that could be depended upon. Christ's Church in America owes more to him than to almost any other officer in the United States Army.

Ministers learn to depend on their prayer meeting members. The prayer meeting is the most important meeting in the church. If your church has no prayer meeting, use your influence to start one. It does not take many members to make a good prayer meeting. You can start with two but aim for many members.

It is wise to have a little group of Christian friends with whom you meet every week simply for prayer. There has been nothing more important in my own spiritual development in recent years than a little prayer meeting of less than a dozen friends who have met every Saturday night for years. We met, and together we waited on God. If my life has been of any use to the Master, I attribute it largely to that prayer meeting. Happy is the young Christian who has a little band of friends who regularly meet together for prayer.

Chapter 10

WORKING FOR CHRIST

One of the important conditions of growth and strength in the Christian life is work. No man can keep up his physical strength without exercise, and no man can keep up his spiritual strength without spiritual exercise—in other words without working for the Master. The working Christian is a happy Christian. The working Christian is a strong Christian. Some Christians never backslide because they are too busy with their Master's business. Many professed Christians do backslide because they are too idle to do anything but backslide.

Ask, And Be Fruitful

Jesus said to the first disciples, "Follow Me and I will make you fishers of men" (Matthew 4:19). Anyone who is not a fisher of men is not following Christ. Bearing fruit by bringing others to the Savior is the purpose for which Jesus has chosen us, and it is one of the most important conditions for power in prayer. Jesus says in John 15:16, "Ye have not chosen Me, but I have chosen you, and ordained you, *that ye should go and bring forth fruit*, and that your fruit should remain: *that whatsoever ye shall ask of the Father in My name, He may give it you.*" These words of Jesus are very plain. They tell us that the believer who is bearing fruit is the one who can pray in the name of Christ and receive what he asks in that name.

In the same chapter Jesus tells us that bearing fruit in His strength is the condition of fullness of joy. He says, "These things have I spoken unto you (that is, things about living in Him and bearing fruit in His strength), that My joy might remain in you, and that your joy might be full" (John 15:11). Our experience more than adequately proves the truth of these words of our Master. Those who are full of activity in winning others to Christ are those who are full of joy in Christ Himself.

If you wish to be a happy Christian, a strong Christian, a Christian who is mighty in prayer, begin now to work for Jesus. Never let a day pass without doing some definite work for Him. But how can a young Christian work for Him? How can a young Christian bear fruit? The answer is very simple and very easy to follow.

You can bear fruit for your Master by going to others and telling them what your Savior has done for you, by urging them to accept this same Savior, and by showing them how. There is no other work in the world that is so easy to do, so joyous, and so fruitful. The youngest Christian can do personal work. Of course, he cannot do it as well as he will after he has had more practice. The way to learn to do it is by doing it.

You Can Start Immediately

I have known thousands of Christians all around the world who have begun to work for Christ, and bring others to Christ, the same day they were converted. How often young men and women, yes, and old men and women, too, have come to me and said, "I accepted Jesus Christ last night as my Savior, my Lord, and my King. Tonight I led a friend to Christ." The next day they would come and tell me of someone else they led to Christ.

There are many books that tell how to do personal work. However, one does not need to wait and read a book on the subject before beginning. One of the greatest and most common mistakes that is made is frittering one's life away preparing to get ready to get ready. Some never do get ready. The way to get ready for Christian work is to begin at once. Make up your mind that you will encourage at least one person to accept Christ every day.

Success Despite Mistakes

Early in his Christian life D.L. Moody made a resolution that he would never let a day pass without speaking to at least one person about Christ. One night he was returning home late from his work. As he neared home, it occurred to him that he had not spoken to anyone about Jesus that day. He said to himself, "It is too late now. I will not get an opportunity. Here will be one day gone without my speaking to anyone about Christ."

Then, just ahead of him, he saw a man standing under a lamppost. He said, "Here is my last opportunity." The man was a stranger, though he knew of Mr. Moody. Mr. Moody hurried up to him and asked, "Are you a Christian?"

The man replied, "That is none of your business. If you were not a preacher, I would knock you into the gutter."

But Mr. Moody spoke a few Christian words to him and passed on.

The next day this man called on one of Mr. Moody's business friends in Chicago in great indignation. He said, "That man Moody of yours is doing more harm than good. He has zeal without knowledge. He came up to me last night, a perfect stranger, and asked me if I was a Christian. He insulted me. I told him if he had not been a preacher I would have knocked him into the gutter."

Mr. Moody's friend called him in and said, "Moody, you are doing more harm than good. You have zeal without knowledge. You insulted a friend of mine on the street last night." Mr. Moody left somewhat crestfallen, feeling that perhaps he was doing more harm than good, that perhaps he did have zeal without knowledge.

Some weeks after, however, late at night, there was a loud pounding on his door. Mr. Moody got out of bed and rushed to the door thinking his house was on fire. That same man stood at the door. He said, "Mr. Moody, I have not had a night's rest since you spoke to me that night under the lamppost. I have come here for you to tell me what to do to be saved." That night Mr. Moody had the joy of leading that man to Christ.

Better To Have Zeal

It is better to have zeal without knowledge than to have knowledge without zeal. It is better yet to have zeal with knowledge, and anyone may have this. The way to acquire knowledge is through experience, and the way to gain experience is by doing the work. The man who is so afraid of making blunders that he never does anything, also never learns anything. The man who goes ahead and does his best, willing to risk the blunders, is the man who learns to avoid blunders in the future.

Some of the most gifted men I have ever known have never really accomplished anything because they were so afraid of making blunders. Some of the most useful men I have ever known were men who started out as the least promising, but who had a real love for souls and worked to win them in a blundering way. Eventually they learned by experience to do things well.

Do not be discouraged by your blunders. Pitch in and keep plugging away. Every honest mistake is a stepping-stone to future success. Every day, try to lead someone to Christ. Of course, you will not always succeed, but the work will still do you good. Years later, you will often find that, where you thought you made the greatest mistakes, you accomplished the best results. The man who becomes angriest at you will often finally be the man who is most grateful to you. Be patient and hope on. Never be discouraged.

Make a prayer list. Pray alone with God. Write down at the top of a sheet of paper, "God helping me, I promise to pray daily and to work persistently for the conversion of the following people." Then kneel down and ask God to show you who to put on that list. Do not make the list so long that your prayer and work become mechanical and superficial.

Prayer Lists And Tracts

After you have made the list, keep your covenant and really pray for them daily. Watch for opportunities to speak to them—improve these opportunities. You may have to wait a long time for your opportunities with some of them, and you may have to speak often, but never give up. I prayed about fifteen years for a man, one of the most discouraging men I had ever met. But I finally saw that man converted, and I saw him become a preacher of the gospel. Many others were later converted through his preaching.

Learn to use tracts. Procure a few good tracts that will meet the needs of different kinds of people. Then hand these tracts out to the people whose needs they are adapted to meet. Follow your tracts up with prayer and personal effort.

Work For Your Pastor

Go to your pastor and ask him if there is some work he would like to have you do for him in the church. Be a person on whom your pastor can depend. We live in a day in which there are many kinds of work going on outside the church. Many of these ministries are good, and you should take part in them as much as you can. Never forget, however, that your first duty is to the church where you are a member.

Be a person your pastor can count on. It may be that your pastor may not want to use you, but at least give him the chance of refusing you. If he does refuse you, don't be discouraged, but find work somewhere else. There is plenty to do and few to do it. It is as true today as it was in the days of our Savior, "The harvest truly is plenteous, but the labourers are few" (Matthew 9:37). "Pray ye therefore the Lord of the harvest, that He will send forth labourers into His harvest" (Matthew 9:38) and pray that He will send you.

The right kind of men are needed in the ministry. The right kind of men and women are also needed for foreign mission work. You may not be the right kind of a man or woman for foreign missionary work, but there is still work for you which is just as important as the work of the minister or the missionary. Be sure you fill your place and fit it well.

Chapter 11

FOREIGN MISSIONS

In order to have the most success in the Christian life, one must be interested in foreign missions. The last command of our Lord before leaving this earth was, "Go ye therefore, and teach all nations, baptizing them in the name of the Father, and of the Son, and of the Holy Ghost: Teaching them to observe all things whatsoever I have commanded you: and, lo, I am with you alway, even unto the end of the world" (Matthew 28:19,20). Here is a command and a promise. It is one of the sweetest promises in the Bible.

The enjoyment of the promise is conditioned on obedience to the command. Our Lord commands all of His disciples to go and make disciples of all nations. This command was not given to the apostles alone, but to every member of Christ's Church in all ages. If we go, then Christ will be with us even until the end of the age. If we do not go, we have no right to count on His companionship. Are you going? How can we go?

There are three ways we can go. We must

employ at least two of these ways if we are to enjoy the wonderful privilege of daily personal companionship with Jesus Christ.

You May Be God's Missionary

First, *many of us can go personally*. Many of us should go. God does not call each of us to go as foreign missionaries, but He does call many of us to go who are *not* responding to the call. Every Christian should offer himself for the foreign field and leave the responsibility of choosing or refusing him to the all-wise One, God Himself. No Christian has a right to stay home until he has offered himself definitely to God for the foreign field.

If you have not already done it, do it today. Spend time alone with God and say, "Heavenly Father, here I am, Your property, purchased by the precious blood of Jesus. I belong to You. If You want me in the foreign field, make it clear to me and I will go." Then keep watching for God's leading. God's leading is a clear leading. "God is light, and in Him is no darkness at all" (1 John 1: 5). If you are really willing to be led, He will make His will for you clear as day.

Until He does make it obvious, do not worry that perhaps you are staying at home when you should go to the foreign field. If He wants you, He will make it clear in His own way and time.

If He does make it clear, then prepare to go step by step as He leads you. When His hour comes, go, no matter what it costs. If He does not make it clear that you should go yourself, stay home and do your duty at home. There are other important possibilities for you.

Go Through Your Gifts

We all can and should go to the foreign field with our gifts. There are many who would like to go to the foreign field personally, but whom God providentially prevents. These people are still going via the missionaries they support or help to support. It is possible for you to preach the gospel in the most remote corners of the earth by supporting or helping to support a foreign missionary or a native worker.

Many who read this book are financially able to support a foreign missionary. If you are able to do so, do it. If you are not able to support a foreign missionary, you may be able to support a native helper—do it. You may be able to support one missionary in Japan, another in China, another in India, another in Africa, and another somewhere else—do it.

Giving Is A Privilege

Oh! The joy of preaching the gospel in lands we will never see with our own eyes. How few in the Church today realize their privilege of preaching the gospel and saving men, women, and children in distant lands by sending substitute missionaries to them. That is, by sending someone who goes for you, where you cannot go yourself.

They could not go if it were not for your gifts.

You may be able to give only a small amount to foreign missions, but every bit counts. Many insignificant streams together make a mighty river. If you cannot be a river, at least be a stream.

Learn to give largely. The generous giver is the happy Christian. "The liberal soul shall be made fat" (Proverbs 11:25). "He which soweth sparingly shall reap also sparingly; and he which soweth bountifully shall reap also bountifully," and "God is able to make all grace abound toward you; that ye, always having all sufficiency in all things, may abound to every good work" (2 Corinthians 9:6,8,9).

Generosity Equals Success

Success and growth in the Christian life depends on only a little more than liberal giving. The stingy Christian cannot be a growing Christian. It is wonderful how a Christian begins to grow when he begins to give. Power in prayer depends on liberal giving. One of the most wonderful statements about prayer and its answers is 1 John 3:22. John says, "And whatsoever we ask, we receive of Him, because we keep His commandments, and do those things that are pleasing in His sight." He received because he kept God's commandments and did those things which pleased God.

The immediate context shows that the special commandments he was keeping were the commandments about giving. He tells us in the twenty-first verse that when our heart cannot condemn us about our stingy giving, then we can have confidence in our prayers to God.

God's answers to our prayers come in through the same door our gifts go out to others. Some of us open the door such a little bit by our small giving that God is not able to pass in to us any large answers to prayer. One of the most remarkable promises in the Bible is found in Philippians 4:19, "My God shall supply (the Revised Standard Version says *fill full*) all your need according to His riches in glory by Christ Jesus." This promise, however, was made to believers who distinguished themselves by the size and frequency of their giving. (Refer to verses 14-18.)

Of course, we should not confine our giving to foreign missions. We should give to the work of the home church as well as rescue work in our large cities. We should do good for all men as we have opportunity, especially to those who are fellow Christians. "As we have therefore opportunity, let us do good unto all men, especially unto them who are of the household of faith" (Galatians 6:10) Foreign missions should receive a large part of our gifts.

Give systematically. Set aside a fixed proportion of all the money or goods you receive for Jesus. Be exact and honest about your giving. Don't use that part of your income for yourself under any circumstances.

The Christian is not under law, and there is no law binding the Christian to give a tenth of his income. But as a matter of free choice, a tenth is a good proportion to begin with. Don't let it be less than a tenth. God required the tithe from the Israelites, and Christians should give the same or more than what God required in the law. After you have given your tenth, you will soon learn the joy of giving offerings over and above your tenth.

Participate Through Prayer

There is another way in which we can be a part of the foreign field. That is by our prayers. We can all go this way. Any hour of the day or night you can reach any corner of the earth by your prayers. I go to Japan, China, Australia, New Zealand, India, Africa, and to other parts of the world every day by my prayers. Prayer really makes things happen.

Do not make prayer an excuse for not going personally if God asks you. And do not make prayer an excuse for small giving. There is no power in that kind of prayer. If you are ready to go yourself, God willing, and if you are actually going by your gifts as God gives you ability, then you can go dynamically with your prayers also.

Missionaries Need Prayer

The greatest need in the work of Jesus Christ today is prayer. The greatest need of foreign missions today is prayer. Foreign missions are successful, but they are not as successful as they could be. They could be more successful if Christians at home, as well as abroad, were living up to their full potential in prayer.

Be specific in your prayers for foreign missions. Pray first of all that God will send forth laborers into His harvest—the right sort of laborers. There are many men and women in the foreign field who should not be there. There was not enough prayer about it. More foreign missionaries are greatly needed, but only more of the right kind of missionaries. Pray to God daily believing He will send forth laborers into His harvest field.

Pray for the laborers who are already in the field. No group of men and women need our prayers more than foreign missionaries. No group of men and women are objects of more bitter hatred from Satan than they. Satan delights in attacking the reputation and character of the brave men and women who are at the battlefront for Christ. No one is subjected to so many subtle and awful temptations as foreign missionaries.

We owe it to them to support them with our prayers. Do not merely pray for foreign missionaries in general. Have a few special missionaries whose work you study so that you can pray intelligently for them.

Pray for the native converts. We Christians at home think we have difficulties, trials, temptations, and persecutions, but the burdens we have are nothing to what the converts in heathen lands bear. The obstacles are often enormous and discouragements crushing. Christ alone can make them stand, but He works in answer to the prayers of His people.

Pray often, pray earnestly, pray intensely, and pray with faith for native converts. We learn from missionary literature how God has wonderfully answered prayer for native converts. It is best to be specific in your prayers for converts and have a specific geographic area about whose needs you keep yourself informed. Pray for the converts in that area. Do not have so many that you become confused and mechanical.

Pray for conversions in the foreign field. Pray for revivals in specific places. The last few years have been years of special prayer for special revival in foreign fields. From every corner of the earth news has come of how God is amazingly answering these prayers. But the great things that God is beginning to do are small in comparison with what He will do if there is more prayer.

Chapter 12

COMPANIONS

Our companions have a great influence on our character. The friendships we form create an intellectual, moral, and spiritual atmosphere where we are constantly breathing. Our spiritual health is helped or hindered by this atmosphere. Every young Christian should have a few wisely chosen, intimate friends with whom he can talk freely.

Choosing Your Friends

Search for a few people around your own age with whom you can associate intimately. Be sure that they are spiritual people in the best sense. Be sure they are people who love to study the Bible, who love to talk about spiritual themes, who know how to pray and do pray, and who are really working to bring others to Christ.

Do not feel at all uneasy about the fact that some Christian people are more compatible with you than others. God has made us that way. Some are attracted to certain people and some to others, and it proves nothing against the others or against you.

Cultivate the friendship of those whose friendship you find helpful to your own spiritual life.

On the other hand, avoid the companionships that you find spiritually and morally harmful. Of course, we are not to withdraw ourselves totally from unconverted people or even worldly people. We are often to cultivate the acquaintance of unspiritual people, and even corrupt people, in order to win them for Christ. But we must always be on our guard with such friendships, lifting them up so they do not drag us down.

If you find, in spite of your best efforts, that a particular friendship is harming your spiritual life, then give it up. Some people are surrounded with such an atmosphere of unbelief, cynicism, criticism, impurity, greed, or other evils that it is impossible to remain without being contaminated. In such a case, the path of wisdom is plain; stop associating with those people to any large extent. Stop associating with them at all except where there is some possibility of helping them.

Books Are Influential

But there are other companionships that mold our lives in addition to the companionships of living people. The books we read are our companions. They exert a tremendous influence for good or evil. There is nothing that will help us more than a good book, and nothing that will hurt us more than a bad book. Among the most helpful books are the biographies of good men. Read again and again about the lives of such good and truly great men as Wesley, Finney, and Moody. We live in a day in which there are many good biographies. Read them.

Well-written histories are good companions. No study is more practical and instructive than the study of history. It is not only instructive but spiritually helpful if we watch to see the hand of God in history. We can see His inevitable triumph of right, and the inevitable punishment of wrong, in individuals and nations.

Some fiction is helpful, but here one needs to really be on guard. The majority of modern fiction is wicked and very morally harmful. Fiction that is not absolutely bad, often promotes false views of life and prepares one more for a fantasy life rather than for reality. The habitual novel reader ruins his powers of keen and nimble thinking.

Fiction is so fascinating that it always tends to drive out other reading that is more helpful mentally and morally. We should be on our guard even when reading good literature, that the good does not crowd out the best. In other words, that the best of man's literature does not replace the very best—God's Word. God's Book, the Bible, must always have the first place.

Pictures Can Shape A Life

There is another kind of companionship that has a tremendous influence over our lives. That is the companionship of pictures. The pictures we see every day of our lives, and the pictures we see only occasionally, have a tremendous power in shaping our lives.

A mother had two dearly loved sons. It was her dream and ambition that these sons would enter the ministry, but both of them went to sea. She could not understand why until a friend called her attention to the picture of a magnificent ship in full sail, which hung in the dining room. Every day of their lives her boys saw that picture and had been thrilled by it. An unconquerable love and longing for the sea was created. This picture strongly influenced their lives.

How many masterpieces with worldly suggestions have sent young people on their road to ruin? Many of our art collections are so polluted with indecent pictures that it is not safe for a young man or woman to view them. The evil thought they suggest may only be for a moment, yet Satan will know how to bring that picture back again and again to bring harm. Do not look, even for a moment, at any picture that taints your imagination with evil suggestions—no matter how art critics praise it. Avoid, as you would poison, every painting, engraving, etching, and photograph that leaves a spot of impurity in your mind. Feast your soul on pictures that make you holier, kinder, more sympathetic, and more tender.

Chapter 13

ACTIVITIES AND ENTERTAINMENT

Young people need recreation. Our Savior does not frown on wholesome recreation. He was interested in the games of children when He was here on earth. He watched the children at play (see Matthew 12:16-19), and He watches the children at play today. He delights in their play when it is wholesome and elevating.

In the stress and strain of modern life, older people also need recreation if they are to do their very best work. But there are pastimes that are wholesome, and there are amusements that are wicked. It is impossible to discuss amusements one by one, and it is unnecessary. A few principles are enough.

Guidelines For Choosing Recreation

Do not indulge in any form of amusement about whose propriety you have any doubts. When you are in doubt, always give God the benefit of the doubt. There are plenty of distractions which are not at all questionable. "He that doubteth is damned. . .for whatsoever is not of faith is sin" (Romans 14:23). Many young Christians will say, "I am not sure that this is wrong." Are you sure it is right? If not, leave it alone.

Do not indulge in any amusement that you cannot engage in to the glory of God. "Whether therefore ye eat, or drink, or whatsoever ye do, do all to the glory of God" (1 Corinthians 10:31). Whenever you are in doubt as to whether you should engage in an activity, ask yourself, "Can I do this to the glory of God?"

Do not engage in any activity that will hurt your influence with anybody. There are amusements, which are perhaps all right in themselves, but in which we cannot engage without losing our influence with someone. Every true Christian wishes that his life would show everyone the best. There is so much to be done and so few to do it that every Christian desires every last ounce of power for good that he can have with everybody.

If a particular entertainment will injure your influence for good with anyone, the price is too great. Do not engage in it. Whether justly or unjustly, the world discounts the testimony of those Christians who indulge in certain forms of worldly amusements. We cannot afford to have our witness reduced.

Do not engage in any activity that you cannot make a matter of prayer, asking God's blessing. Pray before your play just as you would pray before your work.

Do not go any place where you cannot take

Christ with you and where you do not think Christ would feel at home. Christ went to happy places when He was here on earth. He went to the marriage feast in Cana and contributed to the joy of the occasion. "And the third day there was a marriage in Cana of Galilee; and the mother of Jesus was there; And both Jesus was called, and His disciples, to the marriage" (John 2:1-2). But there are many modern places where Christ would not be comfortable. Would the atmosphere of the modern theater be agreeable to that Holy One whom we call Lord? If not, don't go.

Don't engage in any activity that you would not like to be found enjoying if the Lord should come. He may come at any moment. Blessed is that individual who, when He comes, He will find watching and ready, glad to receive to Him immediately. "And ye yourselves like unto men that wait for their Lord, when He will return from the wedding; that when He cometh and knocketh, they may open unto Him immediately. Be ye therefore ready also: for the Son of man cometh at an hour when ye think not" (Luke 12:36,40).

I have a friend who was walking down the street one day thinking about the return of the Lord. As he thought, he was smoking a cigar. The thought occurred to him, "Would you like to meet Christ now with that cigar in your mouth?" He answered honestly, "No, I would not." He threw that cigar away and never lit another.

Do not engage in any activity, no matter how harmless it would be for yourself, that might

103

harm someone else. Someone may be influenced to maintain or even start a harmful habit because our innocent activity was their inspiration.

For most of us the recreation that is most helpful demands considerable physical energy. These activities take us into the open air, leave us refreshed in body and invigorated in mind. Physical exercise, but not overexertion, is one of the great safeguards of the moral conduct of young people. There is little pleasure gained in *watching* others play the most vigorous game of football, but there is real health for the body and soul in physical exercise.

Chapter 14

PERSECUTION

One of the discouragements that meets every true Christian before he has gone very far in the Christian life is persecution. God tells us in His Word that "All that will live godly in Christ Jesus shall suffer persecution" (2 Timothy 3:12). Sooner or later everyone who surrenders absolutely to God and seeks to follow Jesus Christ in everything will find this verse is true.

We live in a God-hating world and a compromising age. The world's hatred of God today may be veiled. It often does not express itself the same way it expressed itself in Palestine during the days of Jesus Christ. Nevertheless, the world hates God today as much as it ever did. It also hates anyone who is loyal to Christ. It may not imprison or kill him, but in some way it will persecute him.

Do Not Be Discouraged When Persecuted

Persecution is inevitable for a loyal follower of Jesus Christ. Many young Christians, when they meet with persecution, are surprised and discouraged. Many fall away. Many seem to run well for a few days, but, like those of whom Jesus spoke, "(they) have no root in themselves, and so endure but for a time: afterward when affliction or persecution ariseth for the world's sake, immediately they are offended" (Mark 4:17). I have seen many apparently promising Christian lives end this way. But if persecution is received correctly, it is no longer a hindrance to the Christian life but a help.

Do not be discouraged when you are persecuted. No matter how fierce and hard the persecution, be thankful for it. Jesus says, "Blessed are they which are persecuted for righteousness' sake: for theirs is the kingdom of heaven. Blessed are ye, when men shall revile you, and persecute you, and shall say all manner of evil against you falsely, for My sake. Rejoice, and be exceeding glad: for great is your reward in heaven: for so persecuted they the prophets which were before you" (Matthew 5:10-12).

It is a great privilege to be persecuted for Jesus. Peter found this out and wrote to the Christians of his day: "Beloved, think it not strange concerning the fiery trial which is to try you, as though some strange thing happened unto you: But rejoice, inasmuch as ye are partakers of Christ's suffering; that, when His glory shall be revealed, ye may be glad also with exceeding joy. If ye be reproached for the name of Christ, happy are ye; for the spirit of glory and of God resteth upon you: on their part He is evil spoken of, but on your part He is glorified" (1 Peter 4:12-14).

A Bad Disposition Can Cause Persecution

Be very sure that the persecution is really for Christ's sake and not because of your own stubbornness, fault, or eccentricity. There are many who bring the displeasure of others on themselves because they are stubborn and cranky. They then flatter themselves that they are being persecuted for Christ's sake and for righteousness' sake.

Be considerate of the opinions of others and be considerate of the conduct of others. Be sure that you do not push your opinions on others in an unjustifiable way. Do not make your conscience a rule of life for other people. But never yield one inch of principle. Stand firmly behind what you believe. Do it in love, but do it at any cost.

Return Persecution With Love

If when you are standing for conviction and principle you are disliked, slandered, and treated with all manner of unkindness because of it, do not be sad, but rejoice. Do not speak evil of those who speak evil of you, "because Christ also suffered for us, leaving us an example that ye should follow His steps: Who, when He was reviled, reviled not again; when He suffered, He threatened not; but committed Himself to Him that judgeth righteously" (1 Peter 2:21,23).

At this point many Christians make their mistake. They stand loyally for the truth, but receive the persecution that comes for the truth with harshness. They grow bitter and start condemning everyone but themselves. There is no blessing in bearing persecution that way.

Persecution should be tolerated lovingly and serenely. Do not talk about your own persecution. Rejoice in it. Thank God for it and go on obeying Him. Do not forget to love and pray for those people who persecute you. "But I say unto you, Love your enemies, bless them that curse you, do good to them that hate you, and pray for them which despitefully use you, and persecute you" (Matthew 5:44).

Remember Your Reward

Anytime the persecution seems more than you can bear, remember how great the reward is. "If we suffer, we shall also reign with Him: if we deny Him, He also will deny us" (2 Timothy 2:12). Everyone must enter into the Kingdom of God through pain and trouble. "Confirming the souls of the disciples, and exhorting them to continue in the faith, and that we must through much tribulation enter into the Kingdom of God" (Acts 14:22). But do not turn away from Jesus for this reason.

Always remember, however fiercely the fire of persecution may burn, "The sufferings of this present time are not worthy to be compared with the glory which shall be revealed in us" (Romans 8:18). Remember, too, that your "light affliction which is but for a moment, worketh for us a far more exceeding and eternal weight of glory" (2 Corinthians 4:17). Keep looking, "not at the things which are seen, but at the things which are not seen: for the things which are seen are temporal; but the things which are not seen are eternal" (2 Corinthians 4:18.)

When the apostles were persecuted, even suffering imprisonment and whippings, "they departed from the presence of the council (that had ordered their terrible punishment) rejoicing that they were counted worthy to suffer shame for His name. Daily in the temple, and every house, they ceased not to teach and preach Jesus Christ" (Acts 5:40-42).

Never More Than We Can Bear

The time may come when you think you are being persecuted more than others, but you do not know what others have to endure. Even if it is that you are being persecuted more than anyone else, you should not complain. It is more fitting to humbly thank God that He has given you such an honor.

Keep your eyes fixed on "Jesus, the author and finisher of our faith; who for the joy that was set before Him endured the cross, despising the shame, and is set down at the right hand of the throne of God. For consider Him that endured such contradiction of sinners against Himself, lest ye be wearied and faint in your minds" (Hebrews 12:2,3).

I was once talking with an old man who became saved when he was still a slave. His cruel master flogged him again and again for his loyalty to

Christ, but he said to me, "I simply thought of my Savior dying on the cross in my place, and I rejoiced to suffer persecution for Him."

Chapter 15

GUIDANCE

I have met many people who are trying to lead a Christian life, but they are troubled over the question of guidance. They desire to do God's will in all things, but it puzzles them to know that the will of God is possible in every situation. When anyone starts out with determination to obey God in everything and be led by the Holy Spirit, Satan tries to confuse that person from knowing the will of God.

Satan often suggests something is the will of God and it is not at all. When the believer does not follow the false suggestion, Satan says, "You disobeyed God." Because of this, many conscientious young Christians fall into a morbid and unhappy state of mind, fearing they have disobeyed God and lost His favor. This is one of the most frequent devices the devil uses to keep Christians from being cheerful.

Knowing The Will Of God

How can we know the will of God?

First, let me say that a healthy Christian life is not governed by a lot of rules about what one is permitted to eat, drink, do, and not do. A life governed by a lot of rules is a life of bondage. One will sooner or later break some of these man-made rules and feel self-condemnation. Paul tells us in Romans 8:15, "Ye have not received the spirit of bondage again to fear; but ye have received the Spirit of adoption whereby we cry, Abba, Father."

The true Christian life is a life of a trusting, glad, fear-free child; not led by rules, but by the personal guidance of the Holy Spirit who dwells within. "As many as are led by the Spirit of God, they are the sons of God" (Romans 8:14). If you have received Jesus Christ, the Holy Spirit dwells within you and is ready to lead you at every turn of life.

A life governed by a multitude of rules is a life of bondage and anxiety. A life surrendered to the control of the Holy Spirit is a life of joy, peace, and freedom. There is no anxiety in such a life; there is no fear in the presence of God. We trust God and rejoice in His presence just as a child trusts his earthly father and rejoices in his presence. If we make a mistake, we can tell Him all about it as trustfully as a child and know that He forgives and restores us instantly to His full favor. "If we confess our sins, He is faithful and just to forgive us our sins, and to cleanse us from all unrighteousness" (1 John 1:9).

Five Points In Seeking Wisdom

But how can we detect the Holy Spirit's guidance that we may obey Him and have God's favor at every turn of life? This question is answered in James 1:5-7, "If any of you lack wisdom, let him ask of God, that giveth to all men liberally, and upbraideth not; and it shall be given him. But let him ask in faith, nothing wavering: For he that wavereth is like a wave of the sea driven with the wind and tossed. For let not that man think that he shall receive any thing of the Lord." The principle is simple. It includes five points.

Recognize your ignorance and inability to guide your own life—you lack wisdom.

Surrender your will to God and really desire to be led by Him.

Have definite prayer time with Him for guidance.

Have confident expectation that God will guide you. "Ask in faith, nothing doubting."

Follow step-by-step as He guides.

God Guides One Step At A Time

God may only show you a step at a time. That is enough. All you need to know is the next step. It is here that many make a mistake. They wish God to show them the whole way before they take the first step.

A university student once came to me with a question about guidance. He said, "I cannot find the will of God. I have been praying, but God does not show me His will." This was in July.

"What are you seeking to know in the will of God?"

"What I should do next summer."

I replied, "Do you know what you should do tomorrow?"

"Yes."

"Do you know what you should do next autumn?"

"Yes, finish my degree. But what I want to know is what I should do when my university course is over."

He was soon led to see that all he needed to know for the present was what God had already shown him. When he did that, God would show him the next step.

Do not worry about what you ought to do next week. Do what God shows you to do for today. Next week will take care of itself. Indeed, tomorrow will take care of itself. Obey the Spirit of God for today. "Take therefore no thought for the morrow: for the morrow shall take thought for the things of itself. Sufficient unto the day is the evil thereof" (Matthew 6:34). It is enough to live a day at a time if we do our very best for that day.

God Gives Clear Guidance

God's guidance is clear guidance, "God is light and in Him is no darkness at all" (1 John 1:5). Do not be anxious about obscure leadings. Do not let your soul be ruffled by the thought, "Perhaps this obscure leading is what God wants me to do."

Obscure leadings are not divine leadings. God's path is as clear as day. Satan's path is full of obscurity, uncertainty, anxiety, and questioning.

If a leading comes and you are not quite sure whether or not it is the will of God, simply pray to your heavenly Father and say, "Heavenly Father, I desire to know Your will. I will do Your will if You will make it clear. But You are light and in You is no darkness at all. If this is Your will make it crystal clear and I will do it." Then wait quietly for God and do not act until He makes it clear. But the moment He makes it clear, act at once.

You Need A Surrendered Will

The whole secret of guidance is an absolutely surrendered will, a will that is given up to God and ready to obey Him at any cost. Many of our uncertainties about God's guidance are simply because we are not really willing to follow God's guiding. We are tempted to say, "I cannot find out what God's will is." The real trouble is that we have found His will, but, because it is something we do not wish to do, we are trying to make ourselves think God wants us to do something else.

God Does Not Contradict His Word

All supposed leadings of God should be tested by the Word of God. The Bible is God's revealed will. Any leading that contradicts the plain teaching of the Bible is certainly not the leading of the Holy Spirit. The Holy Spirit does not contradict Himself.

A man once came to me and said that God was leading him to marry a certain woman. He said she was a very devoted Christian woman, and they were greatly drawn to one another. They felt that God was leading them to be married.

But I said to the man, "You already have a wife."

"Yes," he said, "but we have never lived happily, and we have not lived together for years."

"But," I replied, "that does not alter the situation. God in His Word has told us distinctly the duty of the husband to his wife and how wrong it is in His sight for a husband to divorce his wife and marry another."

"Yes," said the man, "but the Holy Spirit is leading us to one another."

I indignantly replied, "Whatever spirit is leading you to marry one another is certainly not the Holy Spirit but the spirit of the evil one. The Holy Spirit never leads anyone to disobey the Word of God."

Search The Scriptures

In seeking to know the guidance of the Spirit, always search the Scriptures, study them prayerfully. Do not make a book of magic out of the Bible. Do not ask God to show you His will, then open your Bible at random and put your finger on some text taking it out of context and pretending you have seen the will of God. This is an irreverent and improper use of Scripture. You may open your Bible at just the right place to find the right guidance. But, if you do receive real guidance, it will not be by some fanciful interpretation of the passage you find. It will be by taking the passage in its context and interpreting it to mean just what it says as seen in its context.

All sorts of mischief has arisen from using the Bible in this perverse way. I knew an earnest Christian woman who was concerned about the predictions made by a false prophetess. The prophetess claimed Chicago would be destroyed on a certain day. She opened her Bible at random. It opened to the twelfth chapter of Ezekiel, "Son of man, eat thy bread with quaking, and drink thy water with trembling and with carefulness. . . .And the cities that are inhabited shall be laid waste, and the land shall be desolate" (Ezekiel 12:18,20).

This seemed to fit the situation exactly, and the woman was considerably impressed. But if the verses were studied in context, it would have been evident at once that God was not speaking about Chicago, and the verses were not applicable to Chicago. This was not an intelligent study of the Word of God and, therefore, led to a false conclusion.

Free From Anxiety And Worry

To sum up, lead a life which is not governed by rules but by the personal guidance of the Holy Spirit. Surrender your will totally to God. Whenever you are in doubt about His guidance, ask Him to show you His will, expect Him to do it, then follow step-by-step as He leads. Test all leadings by the plain and simple teachings of the Bible. Live without anxiety and worry that perhaps in an unguarded moment you have not done the right thing.

After you have done what you think God led you to do, do not always go back wondering whether or not you did His will. You will become morbid if you do. If you really wished to do God's will, sought His guidance, and did what you thought He guided you to do, you may rest assured you did the right thing, no matter what the outcome has been.

Satan is determined to keep us from being happy, cheerful Christians — if he can. God, on the other hand, wishes us to be happy, cheerful, bright Christians every day and every hour. He does not wish us to brood but rejoice. "Rejoice in the Lord alway: and again I say, Rejoice" (Philippians 4:4).

An exemplary Christian man came to me one Monday morning, dejected over his apparent work failures of the preceding day. "I made wretched work of teaching my Sunday school class yesterday."

"Did you honestly seek wisdom from God before you went to your class?" I asked.

"I did."

"Did you expect to receive it?"

"I did."

"Then," I reassured him, "in the face of God's promise what right have you to doubt that God gave you wisdom?" (See James 1:5-7.)

His gloom disappeared. He looked up with a smile and said, "I had no right to doubt." Let us learn to trust God.

Let us remember that, if we surrender to Him, He is more willing to guide us than we are to be guided. Let us trust that He does guide us at every step even though our actions may not bring the results we expect. Never worry but trust God. This way we will be happy, peaceful, strong, and useful at every turn of life.